FIFTY
FORGOTTEN
BOOKS

ALSO BY R. B. RUSSELL

SHORT STORY COLLECTIONS

Putting the Pieces in Place, 2009
Literary Remains, 2010
Leave Your Sleep, 2012
Death Makes Strangers of Us All, 2018

NOVELLAS

Bloody Baudelaire, 2009
The Dark Return of Time, 2014
The Stones are Singing, 2016

NOVELS

She Sleeps, 2017
Waiting for the End of the World, 2020
Heaven's Hill, 2022

COLLECTED EDITION

Ghosts, 2012

NON-FICTION

Occult Territory: An Arthur Machen Gazetteer, 2019
Past Lives of Old Books and Other Essays, 2020
Sylvia Townsend Warner: A Bibliography, 2020
(with J. Lawrence Mitchell)
Robert Aickman: An Attempted Biography, 2022

TRANSLATION

Le Grand Meaulnes by Alain-Fournier, 1999
(with *Miracles*, translated by Adrian Eckersley)

Fifty Forgotten Books

R. B. RUSSELL

SHEFFIELD – LONDON – NEW YORK

First published in 2022 by And Other Stories
Sheffield – London – New York
www.andotherstories.org

1 3 5 7 9 8 6 4 2

ISBN: 9781913505509
eBook ISBN: 9781913505516

Editor: Jeremy M. Davies; Copy-editor: Linden Lawson; Proofreader: Sarah Terry; Typeset in
Albertan Pro and Linotype Syntax by Tetragon, London; Cover Design: Holly Ovenden; Printed
and bound on acid-free, age-resistant Munken Premium by CPI Limited, Croydon, UK.

All photographs are the author's, save where noted.

And Other Stories gratefully acknowledge that our work is supported
using public funding by Arts Council England.

Supported using public funding by
**ARTS COUNCIL
ENGLAND**

MIX
Paper from
responsible sources
FSC® C171272

CONTENTS

Introduction   9

1 *The Outsider* · Colin Wilson   19
2 *The Hill of Dreams* · Arthur Machen   24
3 *The Most Haunted House in England* · Harry Price   30
4 *Diary of a Drug Fiend* · Aleister Crowley   35
5 *The Other* · Thomas Tryon   40
6 *Devil in the Flesh* · Raymond Radiguet   43
7 *The Tenant* · Roland Topor   47
8 *Two Symphonies* · André Gide   50
9 *Dilemmas* · Ernest Dowson   54
10 *Xélucha and Others* · M. P. Shiel   58
11 *Tales of Horror and the Supernatural* · Arthur Machen   62
12 *Widdershins* · Oliver Onions   71
13 *Lunch on the Grass* · John Sewell   76
14 *Le Grand Meaulnes* · Alain-Fournier   80
15 *A Bibliography of Arthur Machen* · Adrian Goldstone and
     Wesley D. Sweetser   86
16 *Flowers of Evil* · Charles Baudelaire   90
17 *The Salutation* · Sylvia Townsend Warner   96
18 *In Youth Is Pleasure* · Denton Welch   101
19 *On the Edge* · Walter de la Mare   107
20 *The Quest for Corvo* · A. J. A. Symons   114
21 *The Unspeakable Skipton* · Pamela Hansford Johnson   119

22	*The Cry of a Gull* · Alyse Gregory	124
23	*Flower Phantoms* · Ronald Fraser	129
24	*A Little Treachery* · Phyllis Paul	133
25	*Stenbock, Yeats and the Nineties* · John Adlard	137
26	*The Haunted Woman* · David Lindsay	141
27	*The Attempted Rescue* · Robert Aickman	146
28	*The Doll Maker* · Sarban	150
29	*Dromenon* · Gerald Heard	155
30	*Jean Rhys Revisited* · Alexis Lykiard	160
31	*The House of the Hidden Light* · Arthur Machen and A. E. Waite	164
32	*Fireman Flower* · William Sansom	167
33	*Miss Hargreaves* · Frank Baker	173
34	*Sleep has his House* · Anna Kavan	177
35	*The Brontës Went to Woolworth's* · Rachel Ferguson	181
36	*The Fallen* · Dave Simpson	189
37	*The Saint Perpetuus Club of Buenos Aires* · Eric Stener Carlson	193
38	*The Old Knowledge* · Rosalie Parker	197
39	*The Beetle* · Richard Marsh	202
40	*At Dusk* · Mark Valentine	207
41	*Rupetta* · N. A. Sulway	211
42	*The Loney* · Andrew Michael Hurley	214
43	*Copsford* · Walter J. C. Murray	217
44	*The Paris Notebooks* · Quentin S. Crisp	220
45	*Swastika Night* · Murray Constantine	225
46	*The House of Silence* · Avalon Brantley	229
47	*Shadows of the State* · Lewis Bush	235
48	*The Military Orchid* · Jocelyn Brooke	241
49	*The Child Cephalina* · Rebecca Lloyd	246
50	*The Outsider* · Richard Wright	250
	The Hill of Dreams · *A Reprise*	254

INTRODUCTION

Fifty Forgotten Books is intended to be a personal recommend-ation of often overlooked and unloved novels, short story col-lections, poetry and non-fiction. The idea is not just to discuss the books, but to explain what they have meant to me over time, thus forming an oblique, partial memoir of my life. I have been a writer and publisher for over thirty years, and a bibliophile for many more. I hope this volume provides an example of how lit-erature, books and book-collecting have been an intrinsic part of my personal, professional and imaginative life, resulting in friendships and experiences I would otherwise never have had.

The first problem I encountered in my selection was that some of the books I wanted to discuss have never been well enough known for them to be subsequently 'forgotten' – while just as many have always been appreciated, if sometimes by connois-seurs of the less-frequented byways of literature. My title, then, is more a challenge or invitation to readers to determine how many of these works *they* remember. Familiarity with the fifty books I have selected depends not just on how widely read you are, but on simple serendipity, because no book lover can ever hope to work their way through anything other than a fraction of the books they would like to read. A few of my 'forgotten' books are now back in print with small publishers who revive obscure fiction, but at least two have been Penguin Modern

Classics for decades (*Le Grand Meaulnes* by Alain-Fournier and A. J. A. Symons's *The Quest for Corvo*). In my defence, it is often too easy to ignore the classics and assume they are already too well appreciated to be worthy of consideration. For all the prestige of a publisher's 'classic' books, they are invariably heavily subsidised by fashionable contemporary publications.

I was tempted to exchange those better-known books for some that I know are really obscure, such as *The Pepsi-Cola Addict* by June Alison Gibbons (1982), and A *Moving Experience* by Edna Judd (1995). Both would have been examples of intriguing books that few people have heard of, but I thought better of it – in my opinion, they are not actually very good.

Every book discussed here is recommended without equivocation. I have reread many of them several times, and each subsequent reading has usually revealed something new about the book, and also about me as a reader.

It will be noted that I do not only discuss the texts and their authors, although these are obviously the primary consideration. The physical book has always been important to me, and I have mentioned the circumstances of discovering my copies and, where I can remember, who recommended them. A memorable edition of a book, suggested by a friend, discovered in an idiosyncratic bookshop, inevitably adds to the experience of taking it off the shelf again, perhaps decades later. In many ways my book collection today acts as an aide-memoire or diary of places I have lived in and visited, and of friends – even the booksellers who supplied them. Inevitably, in recent years, some of my books have their origins in recommendations online and have been bought from dealers I do not know, simply by pressing a virtual button on a commercial website.

I invariably feel that something is lost by the lack of association, no matter how good the book.

I should explain that my book-collecting turned into a publishing hobby in my twenties, resulting in the formation of Tartarus Press in 1990. I continue to run this small publishing house, issuing approximately ten books a year, with my partner (in life and in business), Rosalie Parker. At every stage, our publishing has been inspired by our joint love of books and writing. It would therefore be odd if I did not include some Tartarus Press books here, although selecting just a few has been an invidious task — we are both passionate about everything we have published.

In my relationship with Rosalie, I am the collector. We 'weed' or 'prune' our bookshelves regularly, and although Rosalie can send books she has finished to a charity shop without a second thought, I always find this difficult. I might want to refer to them, or even reread them. I find that I have to keep the volumes I love, and even 'upgrade' copies for more interesting, often earlier editions. I occasionally find that I can justify owning multiple copies of the same book.

I would like to thank Jeremy M. Davies for commissioning this exercise in obscure books and nostalgia. He asked for a memoir of my 'adventures uncovering rare, strange, obscure books in shops and church sales, etc. of the world'. I hope that I have gone some way to fulfilling the brief.

Perhaps I should say something here about second-hand bookshops today, lest this volume appear entirely backward-looking. Like many collectors, I do of course *look back* with a certain amount of nostalgia to those dusty emporia I visited over the years but which have now closed, remembering the many treasures unearthed in them, as well as the characters encoun-tered. Collectors often assume that there are no longer as many bookshops as there once were, but the literary researcher Mark Valentine recently compared the number of shops in *Driff's Guides to All the Secondhand & Antiquarian Bookshops in Britain* from the 1980s to those still trading today. Surprisingly, he found that, if anything, there are more second-hand bookshops now than there have ever been (if one includes charity shops that deal specifically in books). I can only assume that when I remember the bookshops of, say, the Brighton of my youth (and there were many), they were not all operating concurrently. There *are* still wonderful bookshops in business today. In the last few months I visited Lucius Books in York and came away with a first edition of *Pierrot!* by Henry de Vere Stacpoole, and at Westwood Books in Sedbergh I bought assorted hardbacks and paperbacks including two real gems (Merlin Sheldrake's *Entangled Life* and Alastair Bonnett's *Off The Map*). At Scarthin Books in Derbyshire I found a paperback of *Bruges-la-Morte* by Georges Rodenbach (I had been looking for a copy for ages), and in Camilla's Bookshop in Eastbourne (which still stands after many decades) a splendid Panther paperback of *Cults of Unreason* by Dr Christopher Evans.

Perhaps my most impressive haul was from the Oxfam Bookshop in Ilkley. The highlight there was a copy of Hans Fallada's *Alone in Berlin*.

FIFTY
FORGOTTEN
BOOKS

As a boy, I was a collector, but not, initially, of books. Like my friends, I collected the cards given away in packets of PG Tips tea, sticking them in albums, attempting to put together full sets. I also collected stamps, matchboxes and bus tickets (apparently). I liked to keep the books I read, just as I retained my old comics, but mainly so that I could dip back into them and re-experience the stories. Borrowing from the school library, or the library buried beneath the club rooms in our Sussex village, Horam, was fine, but if I found a really good book I would take it out multiple times for as long as it remained on their shelves (*The Master Book of Spies*, 'written and advised' by Donald McCormick, was a favourite). I could only afford to buy occasional paperbacks from the Scholastic Book Service – usually TV tie-ins like *The Tomorrow People* and later *Blake's 7*. Otherwise, I relied on jumble sales and birthday presents, and books accumulated in the corner of my bedroom along with my comics.

And then I discovered Magpies at the bottom of the high street in our village. At the back of this junk shop, behind the abandoned furniture and unloved ornaments, past rails of musty clothing and boxes of worn but shiny shoes, there were several shelves of tatty books for sale. With my weekly pocket

Magpies junk shop in Horam, 1977, from an old cine film

money of ten pence, and the paperbacks at two pence each, I first found books in Enid Blyton's *Mystery* and *Adventure* series, then the *Biggles* books of Captain W. E. Johns. My teenage reading became quite wide and indiscriminate as I was tempted by exciting cover art, and I went down some unfortunate avenues (the science fiction of E. C. Tubb was one of many mistakes, along with Westerns). I took risks on Edgar Rice Burroughs' Martian novels, Samuel Delany's *Babel-17*, and the low-key thrillers of P. M. Hubbard (*Flush as May*), as well as Mickey Spillane's hard-boiled detectives.

I also started to read some of my parents' books, which were unceremoniously kept in a pile at the bottom of a wardrobe in their bedroom. These were popular blockbusters, from Frederick Forsyth's *The Day of the Jackal* to Alex Haley's *Roots*, from *Shout at the Devil* by Wilbur Smith to Henri Charrière's *Papillon*.

I was never aware that there was a point at which I started to 'collect' books. I was certainly a collector once I had discovered John Wyndham, Ian Fleming and the *Saint* books of Leslie Charteris. Wyndham I loved, buying the 1970s paperback editions with the atmospheric woodcuts by Harry Willock on the covers. I remember being annoyed when I read that Brian Aldiss had disparagingly called Wyndham's novels 'cosy catastrophes', because, as Margaret Atwood later wrote, 'One might as well call World War Two – of which Wyndham was a veteran – a "cosy" war because not everyone died in it.' Wyndham is too well known to need my recommendation, but I always consider his books alongside the remarkable *The Death of Grass* by John Christopher, who ought to be better known. Both authors follow in the tradition of H. G. Wells by writing what should be recognised as a peculiarly British kind of science fiction. There is a certain reticence in the telling, and a focus on an individual's practical attempts to cope with sensational situations. The story often appears quite understated, but this makes it no less effective.

John Wyndham paperbacks, and John Christopher's *The Death of Grass*

The lure of the *James Bond* books was obvious – spies, violence and sex, set in various exotic locations around the world. I rather liked the already dated feel of the original books, which seemed to give them authenticity. The *Saint* books were just as exciting, although I was often wrong-footed by just how old-fashioned some of the earliest adventures were – Simon Templar had a tendency to jump on a car's 'running-board' – a term that had to be explained to me by my grandfather.

These thrilling books were all very well, but after plundering the Magpies stock for a few years, I chanced upon Colin Wilson's literary study, *The Outsider*. I am not sure what first attracted me to the dull-looking Pan paperback, but I think I was looking for direction in my reading. From the inside front cover, I can see that I bought the book in 1981, when I was fourteen years old.

1

The Outsider

COLIN WILSON

First published by Gollancz, 1956.
My copy: Pan paperback, 1963

Wilson's book explores the concept of creative artists who feel alienated from society, using as examples characters from books such as Meursault in Camus' *L'Étranger* (*The Outsider*) and Harry Haller in Hermann Hesse's *Steppenwolf*. Wilson defined The Outsider as an individual on the periphery of society, challenging its values, and living by a personal set of rules. The Outsider, for Wilson, was seeking truth amidst the pointlessness of everyday existence. As a teenager I was a willing existentialist, but I am not sure I ever understood whether Wilson believed alienation was a good thing (in that it enabled the observer to see the world more clearly), or something negative (he also highlighted the rare moments of lucidity and understanding that can occasionally cut through the gloom of existence). Positive, negative, or just inevitable, Wilson suggested that alienation made for some of the most vital and interesting literature, and he brought to my attention Sartre,

Camus, Kafka, Hesse, Blake and Dostoyevsky, some of whom could be found in Pan, Penguin and Picador paperbacks in the same junk shop. I bought them up, and now I knew I was collecting books, keeping them arranged in alphabetical order (by author surname) in an alcove of my bedroom.

I began my first 'wants' list of authors, which I carried around inside Wilson's book, which lived in my coat pocket, becoming progressively more dog-eared, as I trawled jumble sales, junk shops, and discovered for the first time the wonderful world of second-hand bookshops.

Wilson also discussed Barbusse, D. H. Lawrence, Nietzsche and Hemingway, all of whom I tried to read but failed to find of any interest. I was convinced I was an existentialist, but what I was really interested in was twentieth-century European literature.

What surprised me, when I talked to anyone who knew anything about books (mainly bookshop owners), was the low esteem in which Wilson was held. And this is still the view of most commentators today. *The Outsider* had originally been published to great acclaim, and the author was considered a prodigy (this was his first book, published when he was in his twenties, written in the British Museum during the day, as he slept rough on park benches at night). Wilson's essential problem was that he quickly published a vast body of work, and his driven, open and enquiring mind sent him in too many directions, suggesting to his detractors that he gave none of his subjects enough attention. A more reasonable criticism is that he went in various directions that are just too unconventional to be taken seriously (see, for example, his huge *The Occult: A History*, 1971). Does his later work really devalue *The Outsider*? I think not, although I find the book more difficult to read today. I can see, now, that Wilson was no great prose stylist. Sometimes my mind wanders when I try to reread him. But for anyone starting out, wanting to be challenged to take in a wide variety of thought-provoking literature, the book is still well worth picking up and using as a guide.

*   *   *

I began going, every other Saturday, to Brighton with my father. He would drop me off at the railway station and continue on to Hove to watch the football. I would walk straight to the Odd Volume bookshop on Upper Gloucester Road, where I clearly remember buying a copy of *The Naked Lunch* by William Burroughs for a school friend, Bibi Lynch (who has since made a living writing about sex, which was not an option discussed in careers lessons). I was asked in the shop if I was really old enough to read the book (when I tried, I didn't understand it). In 1984, Driff described the Odd Volume in his infamous bookshop guide as 'Sml gen stk Lit & 1sts & leftish'.

I developed a route around Brighton, walking down to the Trafalgar Bookshop, which was rather intimidating, with too many books devoted to sport and multiple leather-bound matching sets. Further down Trafalgar Street was Wax Factor, a much more anarchic shop that sold, as well as books, vinyl records (even more competition for my limited funds). Wax Factor wasn't a pure bookshop, so Driff refused to include it in his guide.

From there I would work my way along the North Lanes, visiting Two Way Books on Gardner Street (always making at least one purchase from the old couple who ran it), ending up on Duke Street. I occasionally found paperbacks in Holleyman and Treacher, but I have better memories of Colin Page's bookshop, which was friendlier and with more accessible stock. The real treasures were to be found in the cellar room that was reached by a clanging metal spiral staircase.

If I had time, I would sometimes go along the Old Steine to a shop that was renamed Tall Storeys, but the only books I remember buying there were paperbacks of Kingsley Amis's *The James Bond Dossier* and Robert Markham's *Colonel Sun*. (I found out later that Markham was Amis's pseudonym. I was pleased that Amis hit the right note – when I later read John Gardner's Bond books, the tone was somehow wrong.)

Noel Brookes

But no matter what route I took around the town (it was not a city back then), I always ended up at Mr Brookes's shop at 12 Queen's Road. (My father would pick me up at a certain time outside the stamp shop a few doors up – he was a collector too.) A small, grainy photograph of Mr Brookes can be found in the furthest recesses of the internet, and it shows the man as I remember him: in a jacket and tie, cigarette in hand, looking wistfully past the photographer's shoulder. His shop was tall and narrow, bursting at the seams, as though passageways had been hacked out from a solid mass of books. On all four floors, the shelves were stacked two or three books deep.

Inevitably, I asked for existentialist European literature and I was directed to the top floor, to shelves on the right-hand side of the window. I have fond memories of sitting in Mr Brookes's old armchair chatting about books and authors with him while he shared a large bar of Cadbury's milk chocolate with me. By this time it was usually dark outside and pedestrians and cars would pass slowly outside in the rain. There was a dangerous two-bar electric fire providing warmth. It seemed to be a calm, cultured place, with violin or piano music playing in the background – never anything bombastic and orchestral, and certainly nothing modern.

I don't know where I heard the rumour that Mr Brookes was ex-MI5 or MI6, and that he had retired on such a good pension that he did not have to make a living out of his business. The story probably came from other booksellers. I was fascinated by the idea of Brookes being a spy – the shabbiness of the man and his shop was reminiscent of down-at-heel characters from John le Carré or Graham Greene novels rather than anything by Ian Fleming or Leslie Charteris. A variant version of the spy rumour was that he was still employed by the security services and was undercover, but this was less convincing. He was believed to have had a knowledge of several Eastern European languages (he was certainly fluent in Polish).

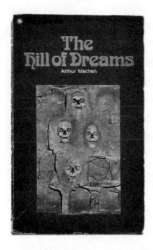

2

The Hill of Dreams

ARTHUR MACHEN

First published by E. Grant Richards, 1907.
My first copy: Corgi paperback, 1967

I shall always be thankful to Mr Brookes for introducing me
to the writings of Arthur Machen. I was talking pretentiously
of existentialism one afternoon, probably trying to make
comparisons between Boris Pasternak's *Doctor Zhivago* and
Dostoyevsky's *Crime and Punishment*, when he handed me a
copy of *The Hill of Dreams*. I assumed Machen was another
existentialist, but the book was so much better written than
anything I had previously read. I still find the opening lines
incredibly powerful, forty years later:

> There was a glow in the sky as if great furnace doors were
> opened.
>
> But all the afternoon his eyes had looked on glamour;
> he had strayed in fairyland. The holidays were nearly
> done, and Lucian Taylor had gone out resolved to lose
> himself, to discover strange hills and prospects that
> he had never seen before. The air was still, breathless,

exhausted after heavy rain, and the clouds looked as if
they had been moulded of lead. No breeze blew upon
the hill, and down in the well of the valley not a dry leaf
stirred, not a bough shook in all the dark January woods.

When I went back to Brighton two weeks later, it was to hunt
for more Machen, but I was sorely disappointed. Machen's
books were hard to find at the time.

On first reading *The Hill of Dreams* I considered Machen's
novel alongside such texts as *Steppenwolf*, and I was surprised when his other writing led me to the genial *The London
Adventure* (1924) in the Village Press paperback, and to the
sensational two-volume Panther paperbacks, *Tales of Horror
and The Supernatural* (1948) (which I enjoyed, not least because
Machen always writes so elegantly).

I 'appreciated' *The Hill of Dreams* when I first read it.
I thought of it as a book about a young man who strives to
write great literature, even at the expense of his love life, and
who descends into madness. Lucian Taylor leaving the countryside, and his beloved Annie, for the suburbs of London
seemed an exile from a land of dream, fantasy and wonder, in
a harsh, soul-destroying city. I knew very little about Machen,
but later discovered that he had been born Arthur Llewellyn
Jones on 3 March 1863 in Caerleon, Gwent, and that he was
best known for his horror fiction, which was described as usually of a mystical cast. *The Great God Pan* (1894) is considered a
classic horror story of the decadent 1890s, and it led me to read
Oscar Wilde's *The Picture of Dorian Gray*. Machen's other work
is sometimes difficult to classify, such as the exquisite 'The
White People' (1904), an apparent stream-of-consciousness

report from a young girl who has strayed into fairyland. What makes Machen's writing beguiling is that when he 'lifts the veil' to show readers what is just beyond our everyday perceptions, the results can be so strange that it is difficult to know if they are glorious or horrific. The discovery of Machen was to have a major influence not just on my reading, but on my career as a publisher. It also helped me make some of the most important friendships of my life.

*   *   *

I must have been visiting Mr Brookes's shop for a couple of years when one day he showed me a collection of film posters he had bought. I looked through them, but was not tempted by any. It was then that he asked if I would like to go back to his flat in Hove for supper. He wanted to show me his favourite poster, which was pinned on his wall. Apparently it featured a strapping young man in a suggestive position under the tagline 'I'm not feeling myself tonight.' He took my refusal very well, and it didn't affect our friendship, but after that I was scrupulous about paying for books rather than accepting them as gifts.

At school I was desperately trying not to be a swot, if not a 'spod', treading a fine line between trying to be cool (I was an existentialist, I was in a band) and being a librarian. A strange, older acquaintance, Michael Kew, persuaded me that volunteering to work in the school library involved very little effort and entitled me to stay indoors during breaks, jumping the horrendous lunch queue. I was put in charge of the 'woodworking' section, which was fine because nobody ever used it, and

I could spend my time hidden away in the library office. The library was closed on Wednesdays, ostensibly so that we could tidy the shelves, but most of my time was spent with Mike, who ran Dungeons and Dragons role-playing games.

After reading *The Hill of Dreams*, I was asking for Arthur Machen in every bookshop I could find, to little avail. I even tried new bookshops, which informed me that Machen was out of print. Second-hand book dealers often advised me to look through the anthologies of horror stories that proliferated either in the darker corners of such establishments or outside on the pavement. In bookshops and junk shops in Brighton and Eastbourne, Heathfield and Hailsham I located odd stories by Machen, but by this means I also came across Edgar Allan Poe, M. R. James, M. P. Shiel, Algernon Blackwood, Edith Wharton, Walter de la Mare and William Hope Hodgson. I ended up owning many battered anthologies, usually with lurid covers. I preferred the collections of classic ghostly stories, edited by Robert Aickman and others, shunning the more modern books and especially the Pan Horror series. I found that I was able to switch, quite happily, between ghost and horror fiction and modern European classics, especially when writing like Franz Kafka's *Metamorphosis* and Gustav Meyrink's *The Golem* seemed to straddle the two genres.

I have a specific memory of buying, one Saturday afternoon at the Two Way Exchange in Brighton, *The Red Brain and Other Creepy Thrillers*, selected by Dashiell Hammett. It cost me only a few pennies because it was such a fragile little paperback, but it had a great cover of a naked woman being assailed by crustaceans. The edges were stained yellow, and it smelt sweetly

Two Way Books, North Lanes, Brighton

of what I now know to have been decaying, cheap paper. My father drove me home via Seaford, where he left me in the car while he went to visit a friend. By the yellowy interior light, I read H. P. Lovecraft's 'The Music of Erich Zann' and I became a Lovecraft fan on the spot. The story commended itself to me because it was set in Paris, specifically on the rue d'Auseil, a street that the narrator could not later find on any map. Like many teenagers, I was seduced by Lovecraft's elaborate language and the hints of forbidden knowledge. I later fell in love with New England, the setting for most of his stories.

An even more important find was the Dover Books paperback reprint of Lovecraft's *Supernatural Horror in Literature*, which now served as my guide, replacing Wilson's *The Outsider* in my coat pocket. Following the recommendations in *Supernatural Horror in Literature*, I discovered in Two Way Books a fine seam of Four Square paperbacks with their green covers, and read Maturin's *Melmoth the Wanderer* and William Beckford's *Vathek*, along with *The Elixir of Life* by W. Harrison

Ainsworth and *The Phantom Ship* by Frederick Marryat. Over a few years the same shop yielded a large number of Lovecraft paperbacks, often in 'exotic' American editions. I don't know why Driff never mentioned this shop.

At Wax Factor I bought 1960s Panther paperbacks of Hermann Hesse's *Demian* and Lovecraft's 'The Tomb', Sartre's *Intimacy* and William Hope Hodgson's *The House on the Borderland*.

For ten years, alongside Penguin Modern Classics, I collected both Machen and Lovecraft with equal zeal. Somewhere on Trafalgar Street in Brighton there was situated a business called London and Brighton Antiquarian Book and Prints. I remember nothing about their shop or stock, though I do recall an enigmatic character called Clive Ogden who undertook a 'book search' for me. My father helped me buy Lovecraft in the bright yellow-jacketed Gollancz hardbacks. However, I soon found that I could never reread Lovecraft's work and recapture the power of that first reading; the overwrought language got in the way. He seemed to be striving too hard for his effects, whereas Machen was always a delight to read and I appreciated his use of language with each subsequent reread.

3

The Most Haunted House in England

Ten Years' Investigation of Borley Rectory

HARRY PRICE

Longmans, 1940

I've never actually owned a copy of this, Harry Price's first book about Borley Rectory. I borrowed it from a neighbour, Andrew Bowler, when I was about fourteen or fifteen, and I can still remember the effect it had on me – the atmosphere it created. Even though I instinctively knew it was all rubbish, Harry Price managed to frighten me. I understood Madame du Deffand when she was asked, 'Do you believe in ghosts?' and she replied, 'No. But I fear them.'

I have always been on the lookout for the book. Andrew's copy had an ugly, utilitarian blue library binding, but I later saw a first edition with its splendidly creepy dust jacket, and I developed the ambition to own that particular edition. It was for sale in Alan Shelley's Bow Windows Bookshop in Lewes (in its old position halfway up the hill) and was priced at a premium because it was in mint condition. I have never come across one since that didn't seem just too expensive.

But I have never seriously regretted not buying *The Most Haunted House in England*, because I seem to recall that it is actually a little dull and repetitious. It is a pseudoscientific account of investigations and events at Borley Rectory, and I may have been guilty of skipping whole chapters when I 'read' it. Not that the pedestrian, detailed, investigative tone made it any the less frightening – if anything, it gave the book a terrifying legitimacy. And the photos! The black-and-white plates of the ruinous building were compelling, not least because at the time my family were looking around some dilapidated old buildings with a view to moving house.

Harry Price is a frustrating character. Commentators since his death in 1948 have generally been critical of his various investigations depending on their own sympathies towards the supernatural. Most agree that he undertook valuable research when it came to debunking false mediums and their ilk, but there is some consensus that he was, at times, prone to bluffing, falsifying and faking. If he can be said to have unearthed any real evidence of ghosts, poltergeists, talking mongooses, etc., he undermined his good work by being guilty, at other times, of outright fraud. One of the most interesting commentators on Price was the author Robert Aickman, who attempted to set up a Trust to save Borley Rectory from demolition and so preserve it for ongoing investigation. (He failed, and the building no longer stands.) Aickman had his own eccentricities and was fascinated by the paranormal throughout his life, but he was too intelligent not to be sceptical of many claims made for the

31

supernatural. Having contacted Price, Aickman visited Borley Rectory on two consecutive weekends, recording what might have been some very minor poltergeist activity. However, he was later suspicious when he discovered that Price had been in the immediate vicinity but had not made himself known. Aickman did not directly accuse Price of throwing a pebble at the investigators, but one can read between the lines. What hurt Aickman most was Price refusing to help with the Trust, only for the great ghost hunter to later lament that nothing was done to save the building.

I have had my own experience of a haunting – a musical ghost at Rosalie Parker's family farm that played three notes on a piano in a recently vacated room. It was not frightening, although it was profoundly puzzling. One of the most important lessons Price's book taught me was that literary ghost stories are invariably far more interesting, readable and thought-provoking than so-called 'true' accounts of the supernatural.

However, through *The Most Haunted House in England*, Borley Rectory lives on, not so much in stories of the ghost of a nun who was apparently buried alive there, or of the spectral coach drawn by two headless men, but in the black-and-white photographs of a very sad-looking Victorian building and its floor plans. The building is, itself, a ghost – continuing to haunt the imagination of believers and sceptics alike.

*   *   *

Apart from fantasies of becoming a pop star, I desperately wanted to be an author. I was writing stories, plays, poetry and lyrics, veering wildly between dour existentialism and purple

The author, aged sixteen, with some of his book collection

Lovecraftiana. In the latter I was aided by Adrian Bott, a fellow enthusiast for Lovecraft. It was Adrian and his mother who introduced me to the music for the *Rocky Horror Show*. He will never let me forget my suggestion that his mother reminded me of Frau Eva, Max Demian's mother in Hesse's novel (which, logically, meant to Adrian that he had to be Demian). Adrian, like Michael Kew, could not quite convince me that Dungeons and Dragons was time well spent.

I had written a Lovecraftian short story called 'The Denizen', which I had published in a home-made magazine called *Mieun* (it was distributed amongst a few friends). Adrian helped me to add even more adjectives and obscure words, and the new version was accepted by Carl T. Ford at *Dagon* just before that fabled magazine folded. An entirely new collaboration, 'Invermorel', was submitted to the Necronomicon Press and was rejected by Mary Michaud, who wrote that the story was 'marred by illogical character motivation', which was indeed an incisive criticism of our story . . . and of all the horror fiction from which it was derived.

In my band, The Trug Concept, with Danny Goring (songwriter and guitarist), we were writing lyrics that tackled such subjects as Franz Kafka's *Metamorphosis*, in a song called 'Gregor'. At this point I was a Goth in everything but dress, listening to Toyah singing about Lovecraft's fictitious grimoire, *The Necronomicon*, in 'Danced', The Birthday Party's 'Release the Bats', and 'Bela Lugosi's Dead' by Bauhaus. As I was self-conscious I only ever dressed up and wore eyeliner once (on a home-made stage on Swife Lane), and I was annoyed that people who called themselves Goths had never read Mrs Radcliffe, Horace Walpole or Charles Maturin. For over a year *Melmoth the Wanderer* had pride of place in my coat pocket – it took that long to read the mammoth volume. But Machen was becoming my literary hero, rivalled only by Edgar Allan Poe.

4

Diary of a Drug Fiend

ALEISTER CROWLEY

First published by Collins, 1922.
My first copy: Sphere paperback, 1972

I have always felt the temptation to buy better copies of books I already own. Over the years I have replaced perfectly reasonable reprint copies with first editions, and then traded those in for firsts in dust jackets, only for a signed copy to come along . . . I try to resist, but my original *Diary of a Drug Fiend*, a 1970s Sphere paperback bought at Two Way Books in Brighton, was well worn by the time I acquired it and only held together with wrinkled, yellow Sellotape.

I was tempted to write here about Aleister Crowley's *Moonchild* (1929), which I have in the Mandrake Press first edition, but it is not a book that I have ever fully understood. My copy, bought from Cummings Bookshop in Lewes in the 1990s when I didn't really have enough money to justify the expense, has the original Beresford Egan dust jacket. It was a smart investment, but I'm not sure that the book is as interesting as *The Diary of a Drug Fiend*.

Crowley isn't a forgotten character, but not everyone who knows of the self-styled 'Great Beast' realises he was also the author of very readable novels and short stories. He is popularly thought of as a charlatan, if not a conman and a sexual predator, but to those who believe in magic he is a towering figure. I have a great respect for friends who take magic seriously, although in many ways they don't seem to be very different from practising Christians I know. (Any attempt at comparing the 'faiths' inevitably results in irritation on both sides.)

Aleister Crowley was an extremely talented man with prodigious energy and ambition, even if it was directed to pursuits that were sometimes questionable. His fiction was often assured and original, and, in the case of *Diary of a Drug Fiend*, loosely based on his own experiences.

The novel presents us with Sir Peter Pendragon, a former First World War pilot of independent financial means, who is lacking direction and is suffering from depression. He encounters Louise Laleham, a follower of occultist Basil King Lamus (a Crowley self-portrait). Pendragon and Laleham fall in love with each other and with cocaine, and the book begins as an unconventional novel of the roaring 1920s. The couple marry and leave for Europe, where they go on a prolonged drugs spree until an old friend steals everything they have.

Returning to London, they end up in a slum, broken financially and in very ill health. The details of their addiction and attendant problems are realistically described, and they survive various vicissitudes. The couple plan to kill themselves by drinking prussic acid, but are saved by Lamus, who aids them in their battle against addiction.

The book has been a well-realised cautionary tale up to this point, where it does something very different. Pendragon and Laleham end up at the Abbey of Thelema, where Lamus breaks their addictions by the use of magical techniques, offering them self-realisation, which allows them to regain control of their lives and destinies.

Diary of a Drug Fiend is a much better book than one might expect. It is entirely reasonable that the novel begins by glorifying and glamorising drug-taking, and it doesn't pull its punches when describing the depths that drugs can plunge addicts into. The book may have been meant as something of an advert for Crowley's Abbey of Thelema at Cefalù, or a model for what he wanted it to be (the reality seems to have been somewhat . . . different). Crowley was a narcissistic egomaniac, but he somehow succeeds with his meandering novel. The book has its faults: the story bogs down from time to time, and doesn't always succeed in attempts to be poetic, but it is told with undoubted

verse. When Crowley's arrogant Pendragon becomes a bit of a bore mid-book, the author sensibly changes perspective to give the previously two-dimensional Laleham a far more interesting role. Crowley might claim that heavy drug use can be controlled if one has the magical powers at his disposal, but he clearly describes the dangers for us lesser mortals. The book is a wild ride; it is a memorable, if sometimes frustrating curiosity.

For anyone who enjoys *Diary of a Drug Fiend*, I would suggest moving on to Crowley's short stories before attempting *Moonchild* (1923). Inevitably, some of his tales are better than others, but I have always had a soft spot for 'The Testament of Magdalen Blair' (1929) and 'At the Fork of the Roads' (1909), initially discovered through my tatty horror anthologies. Inevitably, Crowley came into the orbit of many interesting characters, and there is a wealth of associational material that is well worth reading, such as *The Magical Dilemma of Victor Neuburg* by Jean Overton Fuller, and *The Magic of My Youth* by Arthur Calder-Marshall. Crowley also inspired some wonderful characters, such as the protagonist of Somerset Maugham's *The Magician.* It is even said that Ian Fleming modelled his arch-villain Blofeld on Crowley.

My Collins first edition (no jacket) was sold to me by Anthony Smithson (of Keel Row Books in North Shields) at the York Book Fair only a few years ago. I spent the entire day wandering to and from his stall, taking the book off the shelf and replacing it, undecided whether I should 'upgrade' from my Sphere paperback. Just as I was leaving, Anthony offered me such a generous deal that I could not refuse.

As a cautionary note, though, I would not recommend Crowley's magical writings to anyone who doesn't want to lose themselves in a labyrinth of frustration.

*   *   *

Like many other teenagers in the 1980s, I read popular and sensational mass-market fiction like James Herbert (*The Rats, The Fog,* etc.) and David Seltzer (*The Omen*), while not calling myself a horror fan, because I was also reading more widely.

The only 'big-name' horror novel from this time I still have today is *The Exorcist* by William Peter Blatty, and only because my copy came from the library of the actor Sid James (I can *almost* hear his trademark laugh as I turn the pages). I did keep Thomas Tryon's less well known *Harvest Home* because I felt that it had a slightly different atmosphere to it. *Harvest Home* is a good example of what we now call folk horror – a literary and cinematic genre that has retrospectively co-opted various books and films, and popularly looks to Robin Hardy's film *The Wicker Man* (1973) as its point of reference. As someone brought up in the countryside, I've always been suspicious of the format whereby representatives of 'civilisation' move out of the city and find amongst rural communities folk traditions and pagan survivals (at best), or ignorant superstition and bloodlust (at worst). *The Wicker Man* drew upon David Pinner's novel *Ritual*, which is just about as patronising as the genre can be, and is probably its worst-written specimen (Pinner tortures the English language mercilessly).

I tend to believe that if you want to read proper folk horror you should look for classics such as *The Willows* by Algernon Blackwood, 'The Ash-Tree' by M. R. James and 'The White People' by Arthur Machen. For a satisfying and knowing modern take on folk horror, there can be no better examples than Andrew Michael Hurley's *Starve Acre* or Adam Nevill's *The Ritual.*

5

The Other

THOMAS TRYON

First published by Cape, 1971

Americans have also produced good folk horror, naturally, and Thomas Tryon's *Harvest Home* (1973) is a good example; but I much prefer the author's first novel, *The Other*. My copy, a first edition in a jacket, is probably in the worst condition of any book I own. It was thrown out of the Zetland County Library system (I had no idea where Zetland was at the time, but it sounded engagingly foreign), some of whose stamps are still inside, along with the remains of their labels. It has been read so many times that it is almost disastrously 'cocked' (as they say in the book trade – the spine is at forty-five degrees when it lies flat, so that the front board is at least a centimetre out of square with the rear). Somehow it made its way down to Sussex, where I found it at a school jumble sale and became immersed in it one summer. When I reread it thirty years later in winter in North Yorkshire, I still thoroughly enjoyed it.

The Other is rather more subtle and interesting than the better-known horror novels of its time, showing a real respect for the countryside and those who live in it. Tryon depicts 1930s New England with a genuine fondness that can also be detected in his third novel, *Lady* (1974), a book that, like *The Other*, has a secret at its heart that readers may detect only once they are far into the story.

The Other tells the story of twin boys, Niles and Holland, who live on a farm with a rambling house, a range of barns, fields and a river where they can fish. It is not quite idyllic, for their mother, Alexandra, rarely leaves her bedroom, distraught after the death of her husband. Her sons, although physically identical, have completely different personalities: Niles is caring and happy, while Holland is withdrawn and malevolent. They are both dependent on each other in different ways, and to say much more would spoil the book.

The atmosphere of high summer and tragedy are deftly evoked, and often skilfully described. Take, for example, this description of a dragonfly:

> . . . metallic wings veined with silver and gold, iridescent like fairy-tale wings, inaudibly humming, beating faster than the eye can see. Head loosely jointed, turning every which way, exquisitely sighted eyes avid for prey. Delicate, ferocious little beast, swifter than a swallow, flushing insect game from the clover preserves, devouring, devouring, devouring . . .

Tryon can see the darkness in something as lovely as a dragonfly, and detects a similar darkness in people. *The Other* is, arguably, a clever reworking of William March's more direct *The Bad Seed*.

The Other was a very pleasurable experience on rereading, whereas *Harvest Home* seemed to have dated when I tried it again. I remembered the 'trick' behind *The Other* quite early on, but thereafter enjoyed seeing how the reader is manipulated. With *Harvest Home*, however, I noticed flaws and questioned the attitudes and motivations of the characters. Rereading books after many years is often very revealing of how personal and wider attitudes can change over a relatively short period of time.

6

Devil in the Flesh

RAYMOND RADIGUET

First published as
Le Diable au corps, 1923.
My copy: Penguin Modern
Classics paperback, 1971

I may well have bought my paperback copy of *Devil in the Flesh* from Magpies, but I was always on the lookout for Penguin Modern Classics in their light green livery of the day. I expected *Devil in the Flesh* to be existentialist, but it was something quite different. It has some affinities with Alain-Fournier's *Le Grand Meaulnes* (published in 1913, ten years earlier, and which is much better known, at least in the UK). *Le Grand Meaulnes* is a more subtle and layered book, but both are tragic love stories written by young men who had little time to enjoy their literary achievements; Alain-Fournier died in 1914, a year after *Meaulnes* was published, and Raymond Radiguet in 1923, the same year as *Devil in the Flesh* saw print.

It is a slim volume, which adds intensity to the story of a young man who has an affair with a newly married woman whose husband is fighting at the front in the First World War.

The narrator describes love in its every aspect: from the confidence it engenders to the deep-rooted uncertainties it provokes, from the tenderness it produces to the cruelty, and from the sense of morality it inspires to the amorality it can always justify. Every facet of love is on display and is thoroughly interrogated.

As a young man myself, I was on the side of the narrator. His love seemed to me to justify almost anything, although, even then, I found his self-centredness hard to excuse and his cruelty difficult to understand. Above all, I sympathised with his unfortunate situation, and was as enraged as he was by all the complications and injustices that stood between him and his beloved Marthe.

I am sure that at the time I would have also read Robert Baldick's Introduction, which pointed out that the book had been a bestseller in France. It was originally published with an extensive publicity campaign that was unique at the time: rather than extolling the qualities of the book, the author was promoted and his extreme youth emphasised. This nearly backfired (the critics were scathing about the publisher's campaign), but Radiguet's candour and style brought him many admirers. *Devil in the Flesh* was controversial, though – veterans of the First World War, not unreasonably, believed the book to be a gross insult.

What gives the narrative of *Devil in the Flesh* authenticity is the fact that the author had very recently experienced exactly the love affair that he offered to the public as fiction. Not surprisingly, the publication of the book blighted the lives of the real-life Marthe and her husband, 'Jacques'. Roland Dorgelès, an author who had become a spokesman for the veterans of the First World War, heard from Jacques, who was distraught and wanted to put his side of the story. He annotated a copy of Radiguet's book for Dorgelès, noting with pain where the author had stolen from life and pointing out what he knew to be false.

I recently treated myself to a copy of the Black Sun Press edition (1948) of *Devil in the Flesh*, seduced by the idea of owning a book from such a legendary publisher. (Geoffrey Wolff's *Black Sun: The Brief Transit and Violent Eclipse of Harry Crosby* is well worth reading, even if Harry and Caresse Crosby are not particularly sympathetic characters.) Sadly, the Black Sun Press edition is not a very elegant book, and it needlessly includes stills from a 1947 film which detract from Radiguet's story. Rereading the book recently, I felt the pain of the husband for the first time, even if some sympathy for the narrator still lingered (despite my now being very aware that his troubles are entirely self-inflicted). Nearly forty years after I first read it, I could discern very little of the narrator's love that was noble. What I found most interesting was that the first-person narrative gives us few clues as to Marthe's feelings and motivations, and they would have been far more complicated and painful than those of her crass young lover. The most absorbing books leave the reader wondering what went on before, or after, the events set down on paper. What I wanted from *Devil in the Flesh* was an alternative point of view. It is not a failing of the book, but I want to know more about Marthe because she is, arguably, the central character.

Devil in the Flesh remains out of the ordinary, not least because my perspective on it has changed over time. For a book that is based on real events, it is all about deception. It is a book with many faults, but each is honestly on display. I intend to read it in years to come to see how my perceptions may have changed once again.

Incidentally, my paperback has always had a postcard tipped inside it – an early-twentieth-century street scene of rue Sadi-Carnot, Darnétal, in Normandy. I've just searched online and it appears to have nothing whatever to do with Radiguet or his book. In my mind, however, there is an inseparable link.

7

The Tenant

ROLAND TOPOR

First published as *Le Locataire chimérique* in
1964. My copy: Bantam paperback, 1976

When I came across *The Tenant* in Roman Polanski's 1976 film
adaptation, shown on BBC2 late one night in the 1980s, it had
me under a spell that has never quite worn off. If anything
slightly obscure and interesting ever came on the television it
was unlikely one would ever see it again, so it was wonderful
to discover, not long afterwards, a paperback of *The Tenant* in
a junk shop (opposite the monumental masons) in Eastbourne.
The author was Roland Topor. To my delight the book was
faithful to the film – or rather, vice versa: *The Tenant* had been
first published in 1964 and was filmed by Polanski twelve years
later.

The Tenant satisfied my interest in existentialism *and* horror:
the main protagonist, Trelkovsky, attempts, and fails, to find
acceptance in a foreign city, where his very identity is being
compromised for the convenience of his neighbours. Even
his sexuality is under threat as they attempt to turn him into
the former tenant, Simone Choule. Topor wasn't mentioned

in Wilson's *The Outsider*, and I assumed this was because *The Tenant* had been too recently published.

I will happily accept that the text of a book is of primary importance, but it has always struck me that the aims of the writer and their environment must play a part in any attempt to understand or appreciate their writing. To have known more about Topor when I first discovered the book would certainly have been useful.

Many years later I read that Topor (1938–1997) was an absurdist rather than an existentialist. He was heavily influenced by surrealism, working in various media including illustration, film and theatre, as well as fiction. I realised that *The Tenant* was in many ways a realist novel, and that Trelkovsky is, in fact, a well-integrated member of society – not an outsider at all. If anything, the book is a study in paranoia and mental decline, caused by Trelkovsky's desperation to remain an insider. Trelkovsky is made to change so as to integrate with and appease others, even the local café owner. For Topor, existence wasn't something to question – it was merely absurd – and *The Tenant* explores the absurdity of attempting to fit in with the ludicrous expectations of so-called normal society.

There is undoubtedly a relationship between existentialism and absurdism, certainly as far as their use as literary modes – perhaps the perception of both is a matter of temperament. In some ways my understanding of the book may have altered, but the claustrophobic atmosphere of the apartment building on the rue des Pyrénées, the ill-tempered concierge, as well as the disapproving landlord, remain fixed in their malevolent roles. The feelings of guilt, hopelessness, confusion and despair are all still palpable, and the threat to Trelkovsky's personality remains just the same.

I had always wondered about the denouement of the book, which seemed more fitting for a work of 'horror' than a 'serious' genre. But understanding that Topor was an absurdist means that Trelkovsky's ordeals are all entirely appropriate, and if his end is darkly laughable, it is this that the author wants us to understand about life.

I have never seen the first edition of the English translation of *The Tenant* in any bookshop. They only seem to exist online, where they are horribly expensive. When Millipede Press published a limited-edition hardback edition in 2006 I received a copy as a gift from the publisher, and have kept it, but I couldn't part with my Bantam paperback with stills from the film reproduced on the cover. I have since written an Introduction to the Valancourt Press edition, which means I have three copies. If I ever find a first edition that I could afford, that would mean I'd have four. It remains an ambition!

8

Two Symphonies

ANDRÉ GIDE

First published as *Isabelle*, 1911, and
La Symphonie pastorale, 1919. First translation
by Dorothy Bussy, Cassell, 1931; reprinted as a
Penguin Modern Classic, 1963

After reading so many Penguin Modern Classics, I was thrilled to travel to France with friends in 1983 and 1984. I took a copy of Sartre's *Nausea* with me on the second trip in the hope of spending time reading it while sitting alone outside a Parisian café with a *café au lait*. (I assumed I was too young to order Pernod.) But I never had the opportunity, or nerve, and kept the book hidden for fear of ridicule (I would have deserved it).

It was during one of these visits to Paris, somewhere on the Left Bank of the Seine, that I bought Gide's *La Symphonie Pastorale/Isabelle*. I would love to say that I purchased the book from a *bouquiniste* on the *quais* of the Seine, and in an original French edition. In reality, I bought a second-hand Penguin Modern Classics translation in a hopelessly parochial English-language bookshop that catered for tourists. (I revived the establishment in my novella *The Dark Return of Time* in 2014.) I did not notice the name of the shop, and hoped for many years that it had been Sylvia Beach's Shakespeare and Company. (It was not – I have since visited that famous establishment and it is far more impressive than the shop I patronised.)

I paid too much for my Penguin paperback – something like fifty francs. I did not have the time to read it while in France, but started it soon after I returned home. I liked *La Symphonie Pastorale* well enough, but I loved *Isabelle*. This story (relegated to the second 'symphony' in the Penguin edition) is set in a château in the French countryside, and I pictured it as the gîte in which we had stayed in Normandy. It tells the story of a young scholar, Gérard Lacase, who falls in love with a woman whose portrait he sees fleetingly in a miniature painting, and the set-up is like something from Edgar Allan Poe. Despite the protestations of those who know the enigmatic Isabelle, the romantic hero is stirred by the tragedy of her situation, brought to life in a letter he discovers which suggests that she should have eloped with her lover. This man was killed before they could make their escape, and Isabelle has obviously been banished and is living in poverty, not least because she has given birth to an illegitimate child (who is, additionally, disabled).

The set-up is perfect, but when Gérard finally contrives to talk with Isabelle, as the château and its contents are being sold and the grounds despoiled, he discovers that she has been the architect of her own suffering. Her decisions and actions directly resulted in the death of her lover. She is not the romantic ideal Gérard had dreamed of, but a real woman who has made tragic mistakes. Not only has she had a child outside marriage, but she has had many subsequent lovers.

Isabelle was the first book to make me aware, as a hopelessly romantic teenager, of the implausibility of the unattainable, pure woman. (My varied reading had previously gravitated towards the Poe-esque ideal of the beautiful but dying heroine.) On subsequent rereads, however, I am not entirely sure whether Gide means us to sympathise with Gérard. The protagonist is obviously a fool to lose interest in Isabelle when her story is revealed, and she, perhaps, deserves more sympathy than would have been the case if Fate had simply been cruel to her. My literary education with regard to real as opposed to romantic relationships began with Raymond Radiguet's *Devil in the Flesh*, then *Isabelle*, and continued through to Mauriac's *Thérèse Desqueyroux* not long afterwards.

I have since bought *Two Symphonies* in the first English printing (Cassell, 1931). It is a well-designed hardback that is much more satisfying to read than the Penguin paperback, but I still keep my tatty souvenir of Paris on the shelf alongside it (after all, it cost me fifty francs!).

* * *

I left Sussex for Sheffield University in September 1985, where I began studying architecture with every intention of practising the profession once I had completed my seven years of study and practical experience. By far the most important friendship I made at this time was with Mark Johnson, with whom I wrote songs (well, I wrote the lyrics) which were professionally recorded and released by the band The Bollweevils. I look back on the period with great fondness, not least because my social life was full and interesting, but I didn't really know anyone with whom I could share my passion for books.

I was becoming increasingly interested in the literary scene of the 1890s, acquiring a first edition of Arthur Machen's

The Great God Pan in John Lane's decadent Keynote series, with a cover illustration by Aubrey Beardsley. The 'naughty' or 'yellow' nineties are fascinating, although, like all decades, the characteristics that define it are so wide-ranging as to make accurate overviews difficult. In literature it was dominated by Oscar Wilde, not only by the sparkling and clever froth of successful plays such as *The Importance of Being Ernest*, but also in the darkness beneath the wit of *Dorian Gray*. If the literary decade can be summed up at all, it is in the contrast between the brilliantly gaslit world of the Café Royal, where poets, playwrights and novelists held court while drinking absinthe, and the sordid back streets through which most of them had to return to their inadequate lodgings. Wilde may have lived in some style, but writers like Hubert Crackanthorpe knew the reality of the seedier side of London life and reflected it in their prose. (Not that Wilde's life lacked for such extremes, the doyen of high society becoming its pariah.)

One writer I discovered through reading about Wilde, and who is less often celebrated, is Ernest Dowson. The third stanza of his 1894 poem 'Non sum qualis eram bonae sub regno Cynarae' is impassioned, heartfelt and wonderfully hypocritical:

> I have forgot much, Cynara! gone with the wind,
> Flung roses, roses riotously with the throng,
> Dancing, to put thy pale, lost lilies out of mind;
> But I was desolate and sick of an old passion,
>   Yea, all the time, because the dance was long:
> I have been faithful to thee, Cynara! in my fashion.

9

Dilemmas

ERNEST DOWSON

First published by Elkin Mathews,
1895. My copy: Elkin Mathews
fourth edition, published 1915

Ernest Dowson's poetry is remarkable, but just as powerful are his little-known short stories, collected as *Dilemmas*, first published in 1895. I first came across the collection in 1985 in Alan Hill's bookshop in Broomhill, Sheffield, in my first term at university. I passed the bookshop every day and had been inside several times, but I do not remember making many purchases there. The shop was welcoming, but the books seemed rather too worthy. There was never anything for sale by the authors I knew, and any volume on which I might otherwise have taken a chance was too expensive. I am sure I tried Mr Hill's patience by methodically looking through the fiction and poetry shelves on many occasions.

But just before Christmas, I read somewhere that Arthur Machen had written a book called *War and the Christian Faith* (1918). I didn't expect to find it to my taste, but the title was now a 'want' for my Machen collection and I started to look, for the first time, in the Theology section in bookshops. The quest had been unrewarding elsewhere, so I did not hold out any more hope for Alan Hill's shelves. They were upstairs, in a glass-fronted cabinet under the corner window. It was difficult to read the spines, but in amongst many dull sermons and biblical commentaries there was a slim volume with faded lettering entitled *Dilemmas*.

Dilemmas was seventy-five pence (the price is still pencilled in the front), which was affordable, but I was not optimistic about the contents. Though I knew Dowson as a decadent poet, this was a book of prose, and would have had to be religious, in some manner, if Alan Hill's classification was to be trusted. I knew that Dowson had become a Catholic in 1892, a few years before the publication of *Dilemmas*, but the title page promised 'Stories and Studies in Sentiment' rather than Christian homilies.

I started to read the book while walking up the hill to Ranmoor hall of residence (long since demolished). It was one of those moments when I was completely absorbed by reading, and afterwards I had no memory of crossing busy roads and avoiding other pedestrians. The first story, 'The Diary of a Successful Man', was one of lost love, and at my advanced age of eighteen I already knew the melancholy of mistakes and wasted opportunities in matters of the heart. As I walked through the blackened, sodden leaves that had accumulated on the pavements, in my mind I was in autumnal Bruges with the protagonist, alongside him as he revisited the scenes of a past affair. The second story had a similar set-up: two men are after the same young woman, but she is a Roman Catholic and the sympathetic hero is a divorcee.

The incense of Catholicism hangs heavily over the first two stories, but the book had been wrongly shelved. Dowson's stories are quietly decadent in their beauty and rhythm, and seem to imply that the religious life is no life at all. The stories were perfect for a young man of hopelessly romantic tendencies, who was also a religious sceptic. Rereading the book after three decades, I can still appreciate the quality of the prose and the atmosphere of loss. The later stories are more secular tales of love and lost love, and they are mostly 'pathetic' in the sense of arousing pity and sadness (although the final story now seems to me to deserve the more modern use of the word).

The stories in *Dilemmas* were, no doubt, inspired by Dowson's love for the far-too-young Adelaide Foltinowicz, the daughter of a Polish restaurant owner. Dowson unsuccessfully proposed to her in 1893, and he never recovered from her later marriage to another man. Dowson's life was a short one, full of tragedy – his father died of an overdose in 1894, and his mother, a consumptive, hanged herself the following year. The publisher Leonard Smithers gave Dowson an allowance for a while so that he could write, but in 1899 Robert Sherard found him almost penniless in a wine bar and took him back to his own house. Dowson spent the final six weeks of his life with Sherard, dying at the age of only thirty-two.

After Dowson's death, Oscar Wilde wrote, 'Poor wounded wonderful fellow that he was, a tragic reproduction of all tragic poetry, like a symbol, or a scene. I hope bay leaves will be laid on his tomb, and rue, and myrtle too, for he knew what love was.' (Wilde himself would be dead before the end of the same year.)

The copy of *Dilemmas* I had found in Hill's bookshop was a fourth edition, published in 1915. It is a relatively small book, elegantly set in old-fashioned type, and with generously wide outer and lower margins. Some years later I saw a copy of the first edition at a high but not unreasonable price, and I was tempted to buy it as a replacement – after all, the copy from Alan Hill's bookshop has worn cloth and foxed endpapers. But a fine first edition would not be the same – every time I open my copy of *Dilemmas* it evokes that first time of reading, oblivious of the world around me as I walked up through Broomhill.

10

Xélucha and Others

M. P. SHIEL

Arkham House, 1975

I have never liked defining my literary tastes, because I have always been able to appreciate the subtle, sensitive and sublime writing of Dowson while also enjoying the overwritten and overwrought horrors of someone like M. P. Shiel.

Shiel is a problematic writer on many levels. His short stories 'Xélucha' and 'The House of Sounds' are both remarkably morbid tales, somewhat in the style of Edgar Allan Poe, and when I read them in August Derleth-edited paperbacks from the Two Way Exchange they set me off in search of his other work. I easily found his novel *The Purple Cloud* (1901) (which is astonishing – a very early 'last man on Earth' story), and the *Prince Zaleski* tales (1895) (adventures of a consulting detective so decadent that he doesn't even put down his hash pipe and leave his apartment to solve crimes).

In my first year at Sheffield I sent for the Arkham House catalogue and excitedly arranged for a dollar cheque to be raised by my bank so that I could order their 'best of' Shiel collection, *Xélucha and Others*. A month or so later the book appeared in the post, but I have to admit that I was slightly disappointed by some of the contents. 'The Primate of the Rose' (1928) was another classic story, but most of the others left me cold.

This did not affect the high esteem in which I held the stories I liked, but I later discovered (by comparing them with earlier editions) that my copies had been edited, removing some of the original stylistic excesses. This set me searching for the very first editions through the interlibrary loan system, and I discovered that the originals were indeed superior. However, not all the additional stories omitted from the Arkham selection were up to the mark. Shiel was a very uneven writer, and I had to admit that even the *Prince Zaleski* stories have their faults.

Over the years I have tried Shiel's later work, none of which have held my attention. He wrote various 'romances', several employing the then in-vogue 'Yellow Peril' theme. I was mildly interested in Redonda, a kingdom that Shiel claimed as his own and which the shambling *litterateur* John Gawsworth later inherited. But, like a great deal of Shiel's writing, Redonda was equally unconvincing.

I was interested to find that, for a time, Shiel was a close neighbour of Arthur Machen. Shiel claimed to have been offered (and presumably accepted) the virginity of Arthur Machen's young French maid. However, Machen felt confident to commit to print the statement that Shiel was 'an inveterate liar'.

I didn't go out of my way to find Shiel's first editions. They were invariably expensive, and I find it difficult to let a volume of stories take up room on my shelf just because one of its inclusions is very good, knowing the others to be substandard. But then a good friend, who had fallen on hard times, offered me his Shiel first editions at a mutually agreeable price. I reread *Xélucha*, *The House of Sounds* (1911) and 'The Primate of the Rose' in those lovely editions, as well as the *Prince Zaleski* stories. They stood rereading, an exercise certainly enhanced by the original 1890s bindings (two were in the Keynote series, as two of Machen's books had been). I even bought, from a book dealer in the States, a first edition of *The Purple Cloud*. To my delight it contains the bookplate of Paul Jordan Smith, who wrote an amiable volume called *For the Love of Books* (which discusses Machen).

But Shiel is more problematic than just being an uneven writer – after all, few authors can keep up, throughout their careers, with the standard of their best work. Shiel is more difficult to read since it was discovered in 2008 that he had been convicted of paedophilia in 1915 – of having sex with his twelve-year-old stepdaughter. Added to this, he was unrepentant about it, complaining about the law to the Home Secretary and appealing, unsuccessfully, against his conviction. He served sixteen months' hard labour in prison.

Does the character and private life of an author have any bearing on their work? Some would say not – that the text is the only important thing; but it strikes me as completely reasonable that others would choose not to read Shiel because he was a paedophile. In fact, it is impossible to read *The Purple Cloud* now and not be struck by the youth of the 'new Eve' that the protagonist meets towards the end of the book. It is very possible that in this novel the reader is being invited to share in the author's paedophilic fantasies.

As a collector, one should be aware that rare books can, for any number of reasons, lose their desirability. I am sure my Shiel first editions are no longer as sought-after as they once were. In fact, I'd be happy to sell my first-edition *Purple Cloud*. I've always had mixed feelings about Shiel's other work, but a few of his stories really are successfully atmospheric. It feels wrong to sell *all* of his books, because I am wary not just of literary censorship (which is what it amounts to), but of essentially rewriting the past. To ignore M. P. Shiel and his work would be to forget his crime, and that feels wrong. And I would argue that 'Xélucha', 'The House of Sounds' and 'The Primate of the Rose' are still great stories.

*   *   *

According to my diary, in 1986 (29 April – a Tuesday, to be precise) I went with Mark Johnson and another friend called Pete to see a local band called Pulp at the Maze Bar at Sheffield University. I later wrote in my diary: 'Bloody amazing.' We interviewed the band afterwards, pretending to work for *Darts*, the Sheffield University newspaper. It felt like the culmination of all my interest in existentialist literature to sit around talking with the violinist, Russell Senior, at length about Camus, Hesse and my other heroes. Mark still remembers the evening, not because of anything insightful and interesting I might have said, but because Russell was able to tell us that Camus once played in goal for the Algerian national football team.

11

Tales of Horror and the Supernatural

ARTHUR MACHEN

Knopf, 1948

In September 1987 I was in Providence, Rhode Island with a fellow architecture student, Alex Wall. We were travelling around the USA on Greyhound buses, looking at famous buildings and buying more books than we could carry. We had come to Providence because I wanted to explore College Hill, where H. P. Lovecraft lived for most of his life and had set many of his stories. However, the Lovecraftian spell was beginning to wane.

It was our plan to stay at a hostel the night we arrived, but The Grateful Dead were in town for several days and all available accommodation was booked by Deadheads. While deciding what to do, we walked down the drive of the Halsey Mansion on College Hill, the fictional home of Lovecraft's Charles Dexter Ward, and started talking to the housekeeper, a homesick Welshwoman, who kindly offered us a guided tour of the building. I remember that it had a ballroom, and there was a story about a reappearing bloodstain, but the most notable part of the tour was the cellar, which had a door to underground passages that were said to go down to the river. We only went part way into them because the woman was petrified they would cave in. I don't think we would have been able to penetrate very far, though, even if we had had the courage. I was subsequently told that the old tunnels that Lovecraft refers to in his stories are mere superstition and folklore!

We were very grateful when the housekeeper invited us to stay for several nights. The following day I spent a few hours looking through Lovecraft manuscripts at Brown University Library, while Alex took a trip to Newport. When we met up again late that afternoon we went into a slightly utilitarian Providence bookstore that I remember as being full of metal racking. I was, though, very pleased to find the Knopf hardback edition of Machen's *Tales of Horror and the Supernatural*, which would replace my two paperback volumes of the same name. I also bought a Lancer paperback of Lovecraft's *The Dunwich Horror*.

It still seems terribly ungrateful of me, but in the Charles Dexter Ward mansion that evening, after dinner, for the first time I thought to compare the prose style of the two writers, and found Lovecraft seriously deficient. Machen's prose was sonorous and highly suggestive:

> ... Dyson heard the noise of the brook singing far below, the song of clear and shining water rippling over the stones, whispering and murmuring as it sank to dark deep pools. Across the stream, just below the house, rose a grey stone bridge, vaulted and buttressed, a fragment

of the Middle Ages, and then beyond the bridge the hills rose again, vast and rounded like bastions, covered here and there with dark woods and thickets of undergrowth, but the heights were all bare of trees, showing only grey turf and patches of bracken, touched here and there with the gold of fading fronds. Dyson looked to the north and south, and still he saw the wall of the hills, and the ancient woods, and the stream drawn in and out between them; all grey and dim with morning mist beneath a grey sky in a hushed and haunted air.

Beside this, Lovecraft's prose seemed strained and overwritten. In the very bosom of Lovecraft country, all I wanted was to get back home to reread *The Hill of Dreams*.

As a side note, I ought to point out that at Brown University Library is deposited the infamous poem by Lovecraft, 'On the Creation of Niggers'. This offensive little squib wasn't made public until some time after 2000, although there were already comments in Lovecraft's published stories to suggest his racism (see 'The Horror at Red Hook'). Some apologists for Lovecraft seek to use the 'man of his time' argument, but this is unconvincing – in Lovecraft's own day there were many who would have found his prejudice abhorrent. Additionally, his racism is not unthinking bigotry, as Lovecraft claimed that much thought and research underpinned his beliefs. As with Shiel, Lovecraft should be read today with a knowledge of his views, for they permeate his fiction. It is entirely reasonable that some would rather not read him at all.

* * *

When I finally did reread *The Hill of Dreams* in Sheffield, I have to admit that I felt almost as displaced as in Providence. It made me feel homesick for the Sussex countryside, and I was now even more appreciative of Machen's description of the sunken lanes and haunted woods of the Soar Valley of his youth. I especially valued his evocation of the landscape at dusk and at night. It was at this time that my old school friend Adrian Bott wrote to say that there was a newly formed Arthur Machen Society, and he urged me to join. I had previously kept away from clubs and societies of any kind, but I was frustrated that so many of Machen's books were still eluding me.

In March I travelled down to South Wales for the Machen Society's annual dinner. I left the National Express coach in Newport and walked to Caerleon, passing St Julian's Wood, mentioned in Machen's prose poem 'Nature', recognising the landscape:

> And there was a broad level by the river ... A broad level of misty meadows, divided by low banks, between the hills and the river. They say the Roman world is lost beneath the turf, that a whole city sleeps there, gold and marble and amber all buried for ever.

As I walked, I delighted in the slowly emerging view of Machen's Caerleon-on-Usk – I would spend many happy times in the town over the coming years. It was through the Society that I met friends who helped to shape my reading and publishing life: Janet Machen (daughter of the author, quietly determined and generous), Mark Valentine (an erudite book lover and terrific writer), Roger Dobson (devotee of the overlooked

author), Godfrey Brangham (knowledgeable Machen enthusiast) and Glen Cavaliero (genial critic and poet), to name
but a few. I made a greater number of lifelong friends on that
one weekend than at any other time. And I bought books by
Machen from dealers who were also Society members, primar-
ily Ben Bass and Rupert Cook.

Janet Machen

The Arthur Machen Society had been set up only a few
months earlier by Mrs X along with Godfrey Brangham and
Jon Preece. Mrs X was a born hostess, full of energy and enthusiasm. Godfrey's knowledge of Machen and his writings was
encyclopaedic and his enthusiasm for Machen minutiae has
always been infectious. I immediately liked Jon Preece, and
his friendship has been staunch and was vital during times of
adversity several years later. At the first meeting I was especially

pleased to meet Aidan Reynolds and William Charlton, who had together written the first published biography of Machen. I bought a copy of the biography and had it signed by both of them, as well as by Janet.

Janet was also rather formidable at first, but she, too, became a good friend and an invaluable ally in later times of difficulty. That weekend was my first introduction to Mark Valentine and Roger Dobson, although I did not talk to either at length until the following year.

On the Saturday morning I decided to walk out to Arthur Machen's family home in the Soar Valley with Michael Butterworth, a very tall, softly spoken Mancunian. He described himself as an anarchist publisher – he was fighting James Anderton, the then Chief Constable of Greater Manchester, who had recently put in prison Mike's business partner, David Britton. (Their Lord Horror and Meng and Ecker characters in books and comics were exploring the boundaries of taste and decency.) Janet saw me and Mike with an Ordnance Survey map and told us, impressively, that maps never show you anything of real importance, and she was right – we became lost, and only regained our bearings when we happened across the Farmers Arms in Llandegveth. Here we encountered Iain Smith, although it took ten minutes to realise that he was also a part of the Machenian confraternity.

Walking back to Caerleon with Iain, Mike pulled out of his pocket one of the largest lumps of hashish I had ever seen (I'd not seen many), and, apologising that he had nothing to smoke it with, gave us each a piece to swallow. Soon we were skipping along the road, discussing books, music and the local flora.

Me and Michael Butterworth on the road back
to Caerleon, photographed by Iain Smith

By the time we returned to Caerleon, I had come down from
a very pleasant trip and we all had the munchies. Entering a tea
room and ordering toasted sandwiches, Iain suddenly didn't
feel well and had to leave. Mike and I were in a quandary, but
we paid for the food as it was already being prepared and went
out after Iain. After some minutes, we discovered him sitting
in a builder's skip, and while we were trying to coax him out
someone from the café appeared. They had noticed we hadn't
gone far, and brought out our toasted sandwiches. Iain ate his
in the skip and, feeling better, finally climbed out. We went
back to join the rest of the Society for dinner that evening.

There was an afterword to the story that didn't emerge until
a year later, when Iain was telling other Machen Society members of our escapade. He explained that the tea room had
been decorated bright pink, and that the walls had appeared
to move in and out, as though he were in a giant womb. Mike

and I couldn't remember the colour of the walls, but we were adamant that, despite Iain's protestations, he had not been served his toasted sandwich by a woman in full traditional Welsh costume, including a stovepipe hat.

Mark Valentine and I, 1990, on the Old Dark Lane,
with Roger Dobson behind, photographed by Iain Smith

I attended every Machen Society annual dinner weekend thereafter, as well as later summer gatherings in Amersham, and Michael Butterworth's 'Dog and Duck' evenings in Hadfield. It is to the credit of Mrs X's organisational abilities that we had such a wide variety of interesting and creative active members during her stewardship, from classical musicians (Julian Lloyd Webber), stage performers (Barry Humphries) and record producers (Craig Leon), through to alternative pop stars (Mark

E. Smith), publishers, writers, journalists, artists and rare-book dealers. I felt I wanted to contribute something, so Roger Dobson and Mark Valentine suggested I update and expand their guide to Machen's pubs and places of worship, originally produced as *Taverns and Temples*. I had already bought a couple of their Caermaen booklets, and thought I could do something similar. Their method and aesthetic were familiar to me; this was the end of the old fanzine culture of physically cutting and pasting typed text which was photocopied, the pages folded and stapled by hand. I had tried my hand it at it at school, but Roger and Mark had succeeded in publishing several smart booklets about Machen. It took me a year to research *The Anatomy of Taverns*, and several pleasurable trips to London pubs (some of which have since disappeared), as well as visits to London's Colindale Newspaper Library. Looking back, the booklet I produced was flawed and incomplete, but I have to admire my enthusiasm.

1 2

Widdershins

OLIVER ONIONS

First published by Secker, 1911.
My copy: Secker New Adelphi Library, 1931

I first read 'The Beckoning Fair One' by Oliver Onions in
Bennett Cerf's *Famous Ghost Stories*, published by Random
House in their Illustrated Modern Library. I bought the collection on my trip to the USA, but I don't recall where, and I don't
remember which city I was in when I read it. Most likely,
I was on a Greyhound coach as it travelled up or down the
eastern seaboard of America. All I remember was the intense
atmosphere of the story. The main character, Oleron, rents
a decaying apartment in the centre of London, and as he
gradually loses contact with the outside world he becomes
beguiled by an eighteenth-century spirit. The haunting is
subtle and unique, and I will not spoil it for those who have
yet to read it by giving away the details. All I will say is that,
though I read the story in circumstances that were exciting
and entirely novel to me, I was completely captivated by the
atmosphere of the tale and was unaware of my surroundings.
I should perhaps more appropriately have been reading my

Penguin paperback of Kerouac's *On the Road*, but instead I was immersed in a spooky story set in a dilapidated London square.

I'm also unable to remember where I bought my copy of *Widdershins*, a reprint of Onions's first collection of short stories. It is one of Martin Secker's portable New Adelphi Library books that fit so neatly in the pocket. I have always wanted to replace it with a first edition, but I have never had the opportunity. (Of course, I could buy a highly priced copy from the internet at any time, but where would be the fun in that?) *Widdershins* also includes the stories 'Rooum', 'Benlian', 'The Accident' and 'The Cigarette Case' – all of which are excellent. They cover the whole spectrum of tales, from the overtly supernatural to stories that are more obviously describing morbid psychological states. In this, Onions effectively bridges the divide between the traditional ghost stories of, say, M. R. James and those of more modern writers like, for example, Robert Aickman.

*   *   *

After my three-year undergraduate course, my first real full-time job was as an architectural assistant at the Peak District National Park Authority in Bakewell, Derbyshire. Another employee from Sheffield, Rosalie Parker, was expected to give me a lift to work every day, which did not enderar me to her. It didn't help that when I started I was given some of her more interesting jobs. I immediately fell in love – she was not only very good-looking, but immensely intelligent and interesting. She was one of the first people I met in Sheffield who was as enthusiastic about books as I was, although we also talked easily about films, music and politics. To my dismay, I discovered she was in a long-term relationship.

It was Rosalie who recommended I read Joyce Cary's astounding *The Horse's Mouth* and Lewis Grassic Gibbon's *A Scots Quair* (made up of the three novels *Sunset Song, Cloud Howe* and *Grey Granite*. She encouraged me not to be so defensive about my interest in more obscure literature.

I worked directly for John Sewell, a conservation architect, and I was told by others in the office that he had a reputation as something of a Lothario. This was based on his poetry, which had won a national competition and was published in the newspaper that had sponsored it. The poems were obviously inspired by life, detailing a love affair that some of his colleagues had either known about or claimed to have suspected. The publicity was hard on John's wife. He was regarded in the office with a mixture of awe and suspicion.

I found John to be a charming, easy-going man with strong opinions on aesthetic matters, especially poetry and architecture. It was an intellectually stimulating time – he introduced me to the poetry of Ted Hughes, persuading me that Betjeman (whom I had come to through the poet's appreciation of Machen) was somewhat lightweight. John also gave me useful criticism for a short story I had written, which was to become a published novella and, in due course, was filmed in the USA. John was also very accommodating of my desire to manage The Bollweevils during office hours (I was forever on the phone to venues, designing and duplicating flyers and cassette inserts).

At my request, John gave me copies of his poems. Rosalie had almost forgiven me for causing her so much trouble with lifts to and from work and, as it was summer, on the way back to Sheffield we would stop for ice creams at Calver, or in Endcliffe Park. Sometimes we would have a Guinness at the Grouse Inn.

And I would read John's poems to her and we would discuss them. His writing was painfully honest, juxtaposing frank discussions of sex with wonderful observations of the natural world. Of course, I had ulterior motives in reading the poems to Rosalie, and after a couple of weeks I admitted to her I had fallen in love. She said it would be very difficult for us to have any kind of relationship, but she agreed that she had developed feelings similar to mine. It was a 'difficulty' we overcame.

Rosalie Parker, Bakewell, September 1988

My guide to Arthur Machen's favourite pubs, overseen by Mark Valentine and Roger Dobson, *The Anatomy of Taverns*, was published in 1990. There was a first edition of fifty copies, selling for £2 each. Rosalie photocopied them one lunchtime at the Peak Park Authority offices, and I folded, collated and stapled them at home. It was the first Tartarus Press publication:

I chose the name of the press after a reference made by Machen to Sheffield when he visited the city during the First World War. Because of the steelworks there was no point in having a 'blackout' – the furnaces lit everything up with an unearthly, fiery glow. The steelworkers were on extra wages because of the increase in production for the war effort, and they all seemed to spend their money freely in the public houses. Machen was in awe of the way the steelworkers replaced the fluids they had sweated out by drinking pints and pints of bitter. He considered the city to be a wonderful incarnation of that mythical suburb of hell, Tartarus.

Having sold out of two printings of *The Anatomy of Taverns*, such was my enthusiasm for Dowson's story 'The Diary of a Successful Man' that I drew four illustrations for it, creating the second Tartarus Press publication. It was sent free to all those who had ordered *The Anatomy of Taverns*, which meant that Tartarus Press spent all its accumulated profit and had no capital to finance the next publication.

13

Lunch on the Grass

JOHN SEWELL

The Limes Press, 1989

John Sewell's first collection of poetry, *Lunch on the Grass*, was put together by him out of many of the poems Rosalie and I had read together; some were dropped and new ones were added. As I had already started publishing Tartarus Press booklets, John and I discussed how he should create his publication, under his own Limes Press imprint. It is still impossible for me to read *Lunch on the Grass* with any degree of objectivity. John's poems about love affairs in the Derbyshire countryside didn't exactly mirror my relationship with Rosalie (which we failed to keep hidden from our colleagues – we were spotted together in Beeley churchyard), but they helped create the right atmosphere.

John's first 'proper' collection, *Bursting the Clouds* (1998), was published in the prestigious Cape Poetry series almost a decade later, and there is an overlap of material and subject matter with *Lunch on the Grass*. He has not been a prolific poet, with just a few slim collections published, most recently his fine *Hokusai's Passion* (2020) – thirty-six poems in which there is always a glimpse of the mighty Skiddaw mountain in the background. Over the years I have come to admire his nature poetry more and more, and his more personal work is always powerful because of his acute honesty. *Lunch on the Grass*, though, will always have a special place on our shelves.

Rosalie Parker and R. B. Russell at a party in Derbyshire, 1988

*   *   *

For the first few years, at every Machen Society weekend Roger Goodman, founder of *The Prisoner* Appreciation Society (celebrating the cult 1960s TV series starring Patrick McGoohan), would drive me out to Machen's old house and the church at

Llanddewi. On the third Machen Society weekend in 1990 Mark Valentine also drove me and Roger Dobson to a few other sites in the Soar Valley. On the dashboard of the car, sliding around with an Ordnance Survey map and a packet of Mint Imperials (as Mark negotiated the blind corners and hidden crests), was a Signet paperback entitled *The Wanderer* (1913), by Alain-Fournier. The front cover had an unfortunately 'trippy' illustration of a man in flares and a woman with daisies, but the Afterword by John Fowles was more promising – I had read *The Magus*, courtesy of Magpies.

Mark suggested I might like *The Wanderer*, and the recommendation was seconded by Roger, who pointed out that it was also available from Penguin in one of my revered editions with the

pale green spines. On the same trip, Roger persuaded me to read Mary Webb's wonderful *Precious Bane*.

After the annual dinner, Claire Harman talked about Machen's niece, Sylvia Townsend Warner, and I bought a copy of Claire's biography of Warner. I didn't realise at the time quite how important both Alain-Fournier and Townsend Warner's writing would become to me.

I read Harman's biography first and immediately

went in quest of Warner's books, which were relatively easy to find, and every one was well worth reading. Over a year or so I read all seven of her novels and each was very different from the others. Warner's first, *Lolly Willowes* (1926), is a fine story of an unconsidered spinster who finds some kind of liberation by becoming a witch, but it is the personal revelation that is important, not becoming part of a coven. Even her relationship with Satan is an individual one.

14

Le Grand Meaulnes

ALAIN-FOURNIER

First published in French in 1913.
First published in English
in 1928 by Houghton Mifflin

The Signet translation by Lowell Blair of *The Wanderer* was very good, although the Americanisms grated rather on my English/ European ear. I soon discovered that the Penguin edition was the better-titled *Le Grand Meaulnes*, although Frank Davison's translation was rather stilted. It has since been retranslated very well by Robin Buss for Penguin as *The Lost Estate*. (In its time the book has also been titled and subtitled *The Lost Domain[e]* and *The End of Youth*.) I published a translation of it myself in 1999.

I would not have appreciated Alain-Fournier's novel quite so much if I had read it aged fourteen or fifteen (when I read *Devil in the Flesh*). *Le Grand Meaulnes* is much more a book for the jaded and world-weary twenty-year-old who clearly recalls that time in adolescence when love was uncomplicated and quite innocent, yet could also be erotically charged; when the world could still offer magical experiences not spoiled by common-sense explanations. *Le Grand Meaulnes* is not really a love story; it is complex, although in many ways it makes Gide's *Isabelle* seem very 'knowing', and Radiguet's *Devil in the Flesh* appear almost sordid.

The celebrated event at the heart of *Le Grand Meaulnes* is a *fête*, a party stumbled upon by the hero of the book, Augustin Meaulnes. When he is lost and alone, in the middle of the miserable, frosty and desolate winter countryside, Meaulnes comes across a decaying *domain* or estate and the remains of a château with tumbledown outhouses and overgrown gardens. Despite its near dereliction, it is the venue for a wedding party. All is quite magical and innocent, and at the still, quiet centre of it all is a pretty girl, Yvonne, playing the piano. Meaulnes immediately falls helplessly in love.

In my first reading of the book I enjoyed the quest for the lost party and the lost girl. Without giving too much away, Meaulnes does find success in his quest, but once the girl of his dreams is attained he is off on yet another quest (and leaves his friend Seurel to deal with the consequences). Meaulnes the 'great', the 'wonderful', the 'amazing', the romantic hero seemed to me to be the weaker of the two boys. His apparent determination and courage, once such fine qualities, appeared to be masking cowardice.

This view of the story was reinforced by various commentaries I read, including John Fowles's Afterword to the Signet paperback. I was angry at Meaulnes, the perpetual adolescent who should have outgrown his wanderings and adventures. In the meantime, Seurel had grown into a man, and I felt it was Alain-Fournier's great achievement to reveal that the qualities which allow a person to deserve the title 'Grand' are to be found in those who have fully experienced and moved away from childhood, through adolescence, to adulthood.

When I later came to translate the book myself (painfully, and slowly), I realised that I had originally taken from the text only what I wanted to read. What I had not paid much attention to was Meaulnes's diary, which revealed why he had left – to help another woman, Valentine, whom he had met while looking for Yvonne. *Le Grand Meaulnes* is about much more than the memory of a magical, innocent party, no matter how I remembered my first reading of the book, and despite what some critics have written. The two boys at its centre both move into adulthood as the result of Meaulnes's folly and cruel behaviour in Paris. It is all very well for Yvonne to have said, 'I'd show them how to find the happiness they had never noticed, but which is close at hand,' for Meaulnes was not to know that happiness had been so close. A few miles or several hundred, it was not unreasonable of him to seek Yvonne so assiduously. It was losing sight of his quest for her and taking advantage of Valentine that was his downfall. The 'Grand' Augustin Meaulnes was not so great – perhaps Seurel should never have assumed that he was anything other than fallible and human. What both Seurel and Meaulnes learn, with differing degrees of pain, is that we all make mistakes and that life will add its fair share of tragedy. Whether it is in the magical moment of a childish party, on a seemingly fruitless quest, in an all-too-short friendship or in an intense love, one should value the happiness one happens to possess for as long as it lasts, and wherever it is to be found. Love and friendship are to be cherished for as long as they are available to us.

I have always felt that my translation was something of a cheat. French lessons at school had gone badly and I had forgotten much of the little I knew. I created a new text that was as much a reimagining of previous translations, and based on what I hoped Alain-Fournier had written, than on my understanding of the original. I relied heavily on both a French/English dictionary and Roget's *Thesaurus*. It was reviewed by the *Times Literary Supplement*, who devoted a whole back page to the book. They took me to task over a couple of minor slips, but remarked, to my great relief, that my translation was 'poetic' and had been 'clearly undertaken with affection'.

One of my favourite bookshops used to have a distinctive odour that singled it out from any others. YSF Books (properly, Yorkshire Second-hand Facts) was on the Hunters Bar roundabout in Sheffield in the early 1990s. (They later moved a hundred yards down the Sharrow Vale Road.) In the shop they burned particularly good joss sticks, although I never thought at the time to ask what brand they were, and books bought there would retain the odour for some years. (I am a joss-stick snob and tend to favour Bhutanese incense – I loathe the commercial 'aromatherapy' sticks that smell like toilet cleaner.)

YSF was run by a couple whom I thought of as elderly when I was twenty, but who were probably close to my current age as I now write this and remember them. I didn't know their names, but I have subsequently discovered that the trim, handsome woman who wore black and was unfailingly friendly, even to an impecunious student like me, was called Jimi. Her husband, who had been a GP, was always behind the counter and may have taken early retirement due to illness. I was in awe of them, I admit. There were rather too many books on local history and transportation for my taste, but upstairs was a large fiction section and there was invariably something worth buying. Unlike most other bookshops I have known, where books inevitably accumulate around the owners, I felt that the YSF stock, large and varied though it was, was constantly curated.

I still had slender means, though, and usually had to ration my visits. The shop was less than fifty yards from where I lived, and the temptation just to pop in every day was almost too much, especially when I was alone in the university summer holidays. I know that I bought my Bodley Head *Saki* from there, and Garrison Keillor's *Leaving Home*; one of my most expensive purchases at the time was a curious book by Oscar Wilde called *Sebastian Melmoth*, published by Arthur L. Humphreys. This is a collection of Wilde's epigrams and aphorisms, and the essay 'The Soul of Man'. Mine is a 1908 printing, on lovely laid paper with rough edges, and it was explained to me (by Jimi) that the book was originally published in paper wrappers with the expectation that you would have it bound up to match the other books in your library. My copy is in dark blue half-leather with raised bands and cream vellum. I have come across other copies over the years, all bound differently and always elegantly, which suggests that the convention was quite common, even as late as 1908. I quite regularly take my copy of *Sebastian Melmoth* off the shelf, mainly to dip into the aphorisms, although they don't seem to sparkle as they once did. Every fourth one is marvellous, but there are too many clunkers. Until recently, though, it was worth opening the book just to smell the ghost of YSF incense.

But the book I bought from Jimi that I treasure most is probably *Israfel: The Life and Times of Edgar Allan Poe*, by Hervey Allen. I loved Poe, and had a horrible Octopus Books reprint of his *Tales of Mystery and Imagination* (I later replaced it with the 1923 edition, which did Harry Clarke's amazing illustrations much more justice. Tartarus published an edition in 2018.) When I bought *Israfel*, Jimi warned me that it was not highly regarded, suggesting that Hervey Allen gave up on the idea of writing a formal biography halfway through and instead produced a highly romanticised novelisation of Poe's life. I have to admit that I enjoyed it immensely at the time, and I was impressed by the enormous amount of research that must have been required. I can't defend *Israfel* as a great biography, but I still have my copy, and may well (guiltily) reread it one day.

As a footnote, YSF Books changed premises just as I left Sheffield, and although I subsequently visited the new shop on the Sharrowvale Road many times, it is still the original shop that I like to remember. The curious thing is that although both incarnations of YSF have long gone, their very old-fashioned website can still be found online. It includes a note stating, 'The last book went to a good home on Saturday the 14th Feb 04.' I hope that Jimi and her husband would be pleased that some of the books they sold still have appreciative homes.

15

A Bibliography of
Arthur Machen

ADRIAN GOLDSTONE
AND WESLEY D.
SWEETSER

University of Texas, 1965

When I started collecting Machen, I realised it was not good enough simply to look for his name on the spines of books wherever they might be offered. To obtain more of Machen's work, I needed to know to which books he had contributed short stories, essays and Introductions, and who had written about him in memoirs and books of criticism. And then there were all the articles hidden away in newspapers and magazines . . .

I had heard other members of the Machen Society mention a Machen *Bibliography*, and in the University Library I had gone through the little wooden drawers of the card index system and discovered they had a copy. I was able to find it on the open shelves, and I am not sure that I was allowed to take it out, but I did manage to photocopy the whole thing and I had the pages bound up. This copyright infringement didn't impinge on my conscience because the volume was long out of print, and I thought that Goldstone and Sweetser would sympathise with my enthusiasm. (I later corresponded with Wesley Sweetser, and he did.) This photocopy travelled around with me for several years, becoming increasingly tatty and annotated (not always with bookish notes), before I finally found a first edition offered for sale. I snapped it up. Fairly recently, I upgraded this to a fine first edition inscribed by the main contributor, Adrian Goldstone. (A part of me worries that it is absurd to collect a signed copy of a book compiled to aid collectors. Inside it I keep my correspondence with Wesley Sweetser.)

The collecting instinct is one that has often been analysed and explained, but for every theory there appears to be an exception. It is often said that collections have an emotional value that is of more importance than their monetary worth, but this is not always the case with commodities such as books, stamps, coins, etc. There is also thought to be a psychological importance to imposing order by arranging and managing a collection, but I have known collectors who do not keep anything ordered at all. The thrill of the chase can't be underestimated, but for most collectors the possession of an item brings at least as much joy as the quest for it. Motives and methods of collecting are as numerous as those who undertake the challenge.

Collectors can become needlessly defensive, especially when it is suggested that it is a negative activity, or a childish one, offering emotional and physical support in a world that they are thought to consider unstable and threatening. (Freud believed that all collecting is the result of toilet-training gone wrong!) There are undoubtedly negative aspects to collecting, especially if it becomes an obsession and other important aspects of life suffer (peace of mind, personal relationships, bank accounts, physical storage space, etc.).

For most collectors there are many positive aspects to collecting, quite aside from the satisfaction of making acquisitions. Collecting is generally a sociable activity, as most collectors soon discover the benefits of making personal associations with other collectors, dealers and so on. And then there is the knowledge and understanding of what is being collected. Serious collectors often become experts in their field, even custodians of knowledge that would not otherwise be considered of importance, thus safeguarding and preserving it. Even a completely self-indulgent collection motivated by unashamed nostalgia, given sufficient time, can become historically significant.

The author in Sheffield, 1988

All of which sounds rather defensive . . . I appreciate Goldstone and Sweetser's *Bibliography of Arthur Machen* because it is so thorough and it has enabled me not only to collect Machen's books but to have published him through Tartarus Press and the Friends of Arthur Machen. And I've discovered other authors associated with Machen whose work I've enjoyed, from Edwin Greenwood's wonderful novel *The Deadly Dowager* to Brillat-Savarin's *The Physiology of Taste* (the joy of food!), from Paul Jordan Smith's *For the Love of Books* to the wonderful writings of Sylvia Townsend Warner.

My only frustration with the *Bibliography* was that it contained a number of items that I assumed I could never obtain, including *The House of the Hidden Light* (1904), written with A. E. Waite, of which there were only ever three copies. And the *Bibliography* illustrated Machen's own personal bookplate, which very few collectors will ever be lucky enough to find.

16

Flowers of Evil

CHARLES BAUDELAIRE

First published as *Les Fleurs du mal* in 1857. My copy: Sylvan Press, 1947, illustrated by Beresford Egan

Baudelaire is far from forgotten, as is only right, but the edition I would like to highlight is little-known. I came across the poetry of Baudelaire in a dual-language Penguin paperback from the 1960s, with 'plain prose translations of each poem', and I have always enjoyed the heady mixture of sex and death. In the front of my paperback, I long ago copied a quote originally from *Le Figaro* describing *Les Fleurs du mal*: 'Everything in it which is not hideous is incomprehensible, everything one understands is putrid.' However, I've since decided that Arthur Symons's translation of Baudelaire for the Casanova Society in 1925 is my preferred text, although it took me a while to fully appreciate this. It was only after listening to the band The Sleaford Mods that I realised how perfectly Symons's translation reads if one imagines it being declaimed in a voice that is intentionally angry and trying to be offensive.

But the edition by Baudelaire I would choose if I could have only one is Beresford Egan's illustrated *Flowers of Evil*. Egan (1905–1984) has been described as the 1920s Aubrey Beardsley. Egan's wickedly satirical black-and-white line drawings were perhaps at their most effective in *The Sink of Solitude* (a 1928 lampoon of Radclyffe Hall's *The Well of Loneliness* and a satire of the outraged reactions to her book). Until the early 1930s Egan's brush was delightfully cruel and perverse – he later descended into producing cartoons.

I first came across Egan's artwork when helping Rosalie survey Snitterton Hall, a late-medieval manor house in the Peak District, for her Archaeology master's dissertation. While measuring the attic rooms we noticed a series of wonderfully decadent drawings, all framed, but simply leaning against a wall. On asking the owner, Adrian Woodhouse, what they were, he told us about his friendship with Egan.

Within a few weeks I was in Hay-on-Wye and visited Richard Booth's bookshop on Lion Street. Despite Booth's reputation as a bookseller, he relied for many years on a man called 'Cotters' (I've only recently discovered that his real name was Michael Cottrill). Cotters wore a faded brown housecoat that helped him blend in with the stock, which was piled high and very dusty in those days. When I mentioned Egan he took me into his inner sanctum and offered me a copy of the Sylvan Press edition of *Flowers of Evil*. It was priced £10 on the flyleaf, written within Cotters's distinctive 'Cw' monogram.

Egan was exactly the right artist to illustrate Baudelaire. His drawings of lovely young women and lithe young men are very beautiful and unashamedly erotic, with occasional drapery failing to conceal anything intimate. He often contrasted such figures with merciless depictions of ageing, wrinkled or flabby flesh, but most memorable are the heavy-lidded eyes and world-weary expressions of his jaded libertines. As depictions of decadence, they are unsurpassed. Egan used a brush rather than a pen, and his lines are exquisite.

The first edition of the book was published by the Sophistocles Press and T. Werner Laurie (London) in 1929 in an edition of 500 signed copies entitled, more appropriately, *Les Fleurs du Mal*. I have seen this first edition for sale a number of times, but it has always been out of my price range. No matter – I rather like my copy with Cotters's monogram, although that monogram is not rare.

Booth's bookshop was fundamentally changed about ten years ago when it came under new ownership. The odour of rotting paper and dust was replaced by the smell of wood polish. Nine-tenths of the stock must have been disposed of (along with several hundredweight of cobwebs), while shiny new books at 'remainder' prices were wheeled in. It is, now, probably the prettiest bookshop in the world, although the old atmosphere has been completely lost. However, there are books on the fiction shelves that still contain the flourish of Cotters's distinctive pricing, even though he has been gone for more than twenty years. I was told that he just walked out one day, angry that Richard Booth had not given him due credit in his autobiography.

As an aside, I only met Richard Booth once, at one of the Arthur Machen Society annual dinners, and he was more drunk than I've ever seen anybody who yet remained conscious. I am still not certain that this was an impressive achievement.

Rosalie and I moved to Lewes in Sussex in 1991 when she was offered a job as assistant county archaeologist, and I completed my seventh year of architectural training working for the county council. I became a qualified architect just as an economic recession began, and the only job I could find was working for a publisher called The Book Guild. I should have realised that something was wrong with the business before I had even started on my first day at work. There had been a fire early that morning which had gutted the upper floor of the building on School Hill, where The Book Guild had its office in Lewes. Everything smelled of soot, and there was a pile of charred material at the foot of the stairs. The firemen were still tramping back and forth, bringing it down in armfuls.

As I entered the office I heard the editor, Chantal, saying, 'I heard about it on the car radio coming in and thought, there is a God! My prayers last night were answered. I was so excited, hoping The Book Guild had gone up in smoke. Only, it was the wrong floor that had the fire.'

'So close, yet so far away,' sighed Janet, the production manager.

'We should have wrapped up some potatoes in silver foil and left them up there on Friday night,' said Adrian (who actually produced the books) in his best George Formby voice. 'We would have had baked potatoes for lunch.'

I soon came to realise that working at The Book Guild required a kind of Blitz spirit. I hadn't figured out when I applied for the job that it was a vanity publisher. It offered a very expensive service (averaging £8,000 per book), but my conscience was relatively clear, because the woman running the firm told authors they were very unlikely to become either famous or receive a reasonable return on their investment. She explained they should write off the money and think of the

93

experience as being like a once-in-a-lifetime holiday. However, even with this warning most of the authors had unreasonable expectations of the publicity department, in which I was working, and they caused us a great deal of stress. To give our authors the service they deserved, I was having to sneak back into work after hours to complete tasks that I had promised to do for them. And despite this, there were authors who were upset that their books were not selling well, and others who were downright abusive. I left after two of the most traumatic years of my life, although I had learned how to create proper hardback books, as opposed to booklets.

As a postscript, I did keep in touch with my old Book Guild colleagues and, after I left, the office became even more dysfunctional. They admitted to regularly taking money out of the petty cash to buy bottles of wine to help get them through the long afternoons. And they even made a voodoo doll of the boss, using lengths of her dyed hair plucked from the headrest of her usually vacant chair. To their dismay, the voodoo doll had little effect, but the alcohol took the edge off their despair.

One of the first bookshops from my teenage years that I re-visited once back in Sussex was Holleyman and Treacher on Duke Street in Brighton. A decade before, I had been wary of the two men in suits who looked so much like accountants behind the glass hatch into their office. I suspected them of looking down their noses at me in my leather jacket, and with my obvious lack of funds. They were not unfriendly, though, and the shop was bright and well laid out. I invariably bought interesting paperbacks from them, but I always suspected

Holleyman and Treacher of keeping books from me. Driff, in his *Guide*, had similar suspicions:

> A v lg & unbelievably boring stk, inc the glass case books. V g cond & rsnble prices, rumors [*sic*] of back rm which must be true but I have yet to get invite.

When I returned a decade later, better dressed, with Rosalie and asked if they had anything by Sylvia Townsend Warner, the partner in heavy 1960s glasses respectfully asked me to follow him. We climbed several flights of stairs, past a 'Private' notice, into bookish purlieus that I had always suspected of existing.

The Salutation, in a jacket, was taken off the shelf and offered to me with reverence. The honour of being invited upstairs was such that I could not decline the high price, which wiped out my book-buying budget for a month. But I never regretted the purchase – an overpriced book is invariably better value than most other pleasures at a discount.

17

The Salutation

SYLVIA TOWNSEND WARNER

Chatto & Windus, 1932

It has been said that Sylvia Townsend Warner's reputation as an author might have been higher if her seven novels were not so radically different from each other. Great respect is very often accorded to authors who single-mindedly plough similar, if not the same furrows. However, Warner's novels do have certain recurring characteristics that are shared with most of her short stories. Despite the author's relatively privileged background, all her writing considers the position of apparently ordinary and overlooked people in society, treating them with compassion and revealing how extraordinary they can often be.

Thirty years ago I might have been able to argue that Sylvia Townsend Warner was 'forgotten', even though Virago was keeping her novels intermittently in print. *Lolly Willowes* has been almost continually available since it was first published in 1926, and it is considered by many to be her best book. It can be read as a commentary on the place of single women in 1920s society, although, as with any really good writing, it resonates with sympathetic readers on many other levels.

Sylvia Townsend Warner spent just as much time writing short stories as novels, and because she was a favourite of the *New Yorker* magazine from the 1930s through to the 1970s, she was able to make a living out of them. However, very few authors are acclaimed for their short stories. This form of snobbery is as entrenched in the world of academia as it is in commercial bookselling. Novels are not only considered to be more impressive as works of literature, but they are meant to sell better. One way of exploding the myth of the relative importance of the novel is by considering how many out of the hundreds of thousands published every year are worth remembering. Sylvia Townsend Warner wrote short stories that were as much of a literary achievement as her longer works.

Perhaps her best short stories were collected in *The Salutation*. Her writing at the time of its publication was shaped by her meeting with and reverence for T. F. Powys. 'TFP' was an interesting yet awkward writer; Warner purloined his rural characters and backgrounds, adding the craft of a born story-teller, removing the ever-present, angular and curmudgeonly God of Powys's work and replacing him with secular compassion. The highlight of the collection is 'The Salutation' itself, which is actually a novella (an even more maligned form than the short story). 'The Salutation' is a quiet but powerful elegy to sadness and loss. Although the reader does not need to know this, 'The Salutation' is a sequel to her novel *Mr Fortune's Maggot* (1927).

Warner is dextrous in delineating character and place, often through carefully chosen domestic or small-scale detail. She is skilled in creating appropriate and apposite metaphors and allusions, although she sometimes comes close to 'over-egging' her puddings.

Warner's politics were very much to the left. Her biographer, Claire Harman, attributes Warner's membership of the Communist Party in the 1930s to the rise of fascism in Europe, and it was not until late in life that Warner allowed her membership to lapse. Warner was rather more forgiving of Stalin than history can justify. She had a romantic attachment to communism that can be explained by her compassion for others – a compassion that makes her writing so insightful.

Later stories share the characteristics of these early examples, but at some point in her career she acquired a 'fatal facility'. The stories become entertainments, written for a particular audience – specifically for her 'gentleman friend', the *New Yorker*. One wishes that she had written a few more novellas like 'The Salutation', in which her imagination could have been allowed to stretch out to a length appropriate to the story, rather than accommodating the demands of a transatlantic editor.

After Holleyman and Treacher, I took Rosalie along to see Mr Brookes, to find that he had just opened another shop directly opposite his old one. It was a huge, modern double unit with endless empty shelves. And there were large glass-fronted cabinets down one long wall. It struck me as utterly wrong, and I had visions of tidiness, cleanliness and order being imposed on his unruly stock. When we returned the following year we found that the apparent chaos and confusion of the old shop had simply been transferred to the new one. Not only were the shelves overflowing, but there were bags and boxes up against the windows and cabinets, and clogging the aisles. I don't know where all this stock had come from, because the old shop was operating simultaneously over the road.

But if the pandemonium of the old shop had infected the new one, little of the charm had been transferred with it. Of course, this may be nostalgia, but the lovable eccentricity of the original shop was more akin to madness in the new premises. Mr Brookes was no longer quite so friendly, and his air of mystery also seemed to have disappeared. However, the final months of his business were in keeping with the enigmatic man I had first known.

In the Brighton *Evening Argus* in July 2002 was the story 'Final chapter for chaotic bookshop'. It stated:

> The books are piled high and scattered randomly, as they have been for 30 years . . . Now, though, the doors are locked, Mr Brookes has not been seen and the abandoned books are being farmed out to other second-hand stores. Landlord Nigel Collins has not heard from Mr Brookes for three months, nor received rent for the property in Queens Road, Brighton. All attempts to contact him have failed. Mr Collins has been forced to shut the shop and has started selling the books to shops in central London. Fellow shopkeepers in Queens Road are baffled by the sudden disappearance of a man they regularly saw but never really knew.

There had been a fifty per cent sale, followed by a seventy-five per cent sale, before the doors had been locked for the last time. In November 2002 the *Argus* reported:

Noel Brookes mysteriously deserted his bookshop in Queens Road earlier this year, after 30 years in charge. After trying in vain to contact Mr Brookes, landlord Nigel Collins decided to throw open the chaotic store and let people take what they wanted. The whereabouts of Mr Brookes are still unknown.

John Shire wrote in *Bookends* (2011) that despite the suggestion that Brookes had disappeared, he occasionally saw him

... striding purposefully around Brighton with Sainsbury's shopping bags ... Other dealers remained in contact ... Brookes died in early 2008. His personal effects were dealt with by the arrival of a long-estranged and previously unseen brother.

Quite what Mr Brookes had been doing between 2002 and 2008 is a mystery, and that is how it should be. I like to think that some unspecified government agency called him out of retirement to undertake a clandestine assignment in Eastern Europe. I now wish I had talked with him about Ian Fleming and books about spies – my first bookish interest – because he might have let something slip.

The local newspaper reported that Mr Brookes died in Hove, so I assume that he returned home safely, mission accomplished. The mysterious brother, undoubtedly, was a fellow 'spook', making sure that there was nothing left behind to show who N. F. Brookes had really been working for.

18

In Youth Is Pleasure

DENTON WELCH

Routledge, 1944

Denton Welch would have thought it entirely appropriate that I bought my copy of his book, *In Youth Is Pleasure*, at The Lilies in Weedon, near Aylesbury. While staying with Rosalie's family near Thame, I had looked up 'Bookshops' in *The Yellow Pages* and driven out to the village expecting to find something resembling commercial retail premises. Of course, some 'bookshops' are to be found in anonymous terraced houses, or even in barns down farm tracks, but the only sign in the village for The Lilies indicated a very large, private mansion. It was after ten minutes of scratching my head that I risked driving through the gate and parking on the expanse of gravel around the back, under the imposing rear elevation. I knocked warily on the door to ask for directions, and was told that this was 'the shop'.

On entering The Lilies the book collector was handed a plan of the house. It showed which rooms were available to the public (not all of them had books in – some contained displays of china and paintings, I recall). On my first visit I confined myself to the general stock for sale in a series of attic rooms. There were also a few glass cases up there, under the roof, that acted as a very idiosyncratic museum, containing, amongst other items, John Cowper's death mask.

It was in the attic that I located a copy of *In Youth Is Pleasure* priced at £2. Welch had been recommended to me by Mark Valentine, and many of his other recommendations had been good ones.

After perhaps an hour, a member of staff appeared to ask if I would like a tea or a coffee. I gratefully accepted tea and said I would follow them down, but it was explained that a bell would ring when it was ready. I was also told in which room it would be served.

The bell summoned me to a large and gracefully appointed drawing room where my tea was waiting in a bone china cup, with a plate of digestive biscuits, on a tray. I sat reading Denton Welch while enjoying the refreshments, convinced that my hosts had mistaken me for somebody else.

In Youth Is Pleasure starts with young Orville Pym staying in a hotel that was once a country house and, inevitably, I pictured it as The Lilies. Mark Valentine has written of Welch:

... even when he is simply telling us about what he had to eat for a picnic, or the sometimes rather dingy individuals he has met while out walking, his eye for the telling detail and his turn of phrase make every moment a pleasure to read.

I was captivated. Time seems to stand still when reading Welch – one enters a perfectly realised and heartfelt world. He brings scenes to life as an illustrator does, offering exactly the right details in apparently unaffected and calm prose. Welch was never more at home than when in a dusty old antique shop on the lookout for treasures, and in his prose he offers events, people and places with the genuine delight of a collector, albeit an impecunious one who has discovered items that are interesting and lovely, without being anything to interest serious connoisseurs. His examples are often slightly imperfect, rubbed or worn, like a beautifully decorated saucer that is the only survivor of a grand dinner service. He sees in such items both beauty and sadness, and communicates this to his readers.

I still have a great affection for this book, although I tend to think that his first book, the autobiographical *Maiden Voyage* (1943), is a better one. Every now and again the omniscient narrator of *In Youth Is Pleasure* stumbles and moves close to the territory of Daisy Ashford's *The Young Visiters*. However, Welch's joy and wonder at everything, and his fascination for unlikely specifics, invariably saves him.

I never met the original owner of The Lilies, Peter Eaton, but I did meet his widow, Margaret. Memorably, and painfully, I discovered there a shelf full of Sylvia Townsend Warner's books, including a number of rarities that I had never seen before. At the time I was compiling a bibliography of Warner's works, and I was excitedly making a pile of choice items when Mrs Eaton told me that they were not yet for sale. She had only just bought them, and required time to price them. It was suggested that I come back another day. I insisted on leaving her my name, phone number and address, making her promise to contact me as soon as they were available. Over the next few months I telephoned regularly, but to no avail – she had still not found time to look at them. When I was next able to visit, it was too late. They had already been priced, and the shelf had just been plundered by somebody who knew exactly what was rare. It took another twenty years to find the books I had missed out on, and my *Bibliography* was not published until 2020.

I bought *Uncle Stephen* by Forrest Reid in a little second-hand bookshop near Euston railway station. Working for The Book Guild, I would go to up to London once a month for a meeting in the morning and then have the afternoon free. I tried to visit different bookshops every time. In this particular shop I remember there being an atmosphere like syrup, or liquid amber. Perhaps it was just a dark winter afternoon and the lights were on. I also remember there being too many gilt-tooled leather bindings, and a complete indifference to customer service. When I mentioned to the proprietor which authors I collected, I was casually passed a small Sylvia Townsend Warner booklet, a real rarity, for very little money. In fact, it was a similar price (£3.50) to the copy of *Uncle Stephen* that I bought at the same time. When I tried to find the shop again only a few months later, it seemed to have disappeared.

I know I read the Sylvia Townsend Warner booklet on the train on the way home, but I have no memory of where I read Forrest Reid's book. The grounds of Uncle Stephen's house and the surrounding Ulster countryside are a memorably atmospheric world all of their own. The book incorporates elements of time travel and magic but is, at heart, about the joys and responsibilities of friendship. It has affinities not only with the Gothic but also with more sensitive coming-of-age novels. Reid uses evocative descriptions of nature to entice the reader into a world that apparently came to him in a dream.

I first encountered the book dealer George Locke in his cellar room in a bookshop in Cecil Court, where he was dozing in a chair with his stock piled up about him – books appeared to have drifted around his periphery in that way they do in some bookshops, blurring the edges of a room, even hiding smaller items of furniture, or customers. I had to wake him up to ask the price of a jacketed copy of Beresford Egan's *But the Sinners Triumph*.

'Sixty-five pounds,' he declared. I had nothing like that much money to spend, especially as I didn't know whether I would enjoy the book. I loved Egan's drawings in *The Sink of Solitude* and *Policeman of the Lord*, but by the time of his first novel, *Pollen*, the deft, cruel line of Egan's artwork had deteriorated, and the illustrations in *But the Sinners Triumph* looked even less convincing.

I quickly realised that Mr Locke was a mine of information on supernatural, strange and weird literature. He talked knowledgeably about William Hope Hodgson, M. R. James and H. P. Lovecraft. I proudly admitted that the large parcel I was carrying contained five copies of the newly published Tartarus Press edition of *Ritual and Other Stories* by Arthur Machen (originally published in 1936). I was hoping to drop them off at Smail's Legal Deposit Office on Euston Street (to save the postage, which was considerable). George then proposed I exchange those five copies of *Ritual* (which, as editor and publisher,

105

I would sign) for the book by Egan. I found myself agreeing, even though he explained that I would have to give him a generous discount because he was in the trade. Additionally, he was buying in bulk, and on top of this he was saving me the postage of sending him the books. I, however, was not entitled to any discount because I admitted I was buying the Egan for my collection. When I later paid to have another five copies of *Ritual* bound up and posted to Smail I realised just how out of pocket I had been in my deal with George. To add insult to injury, he was selling my copies of *Ritual* at more than the retail price because (as he explained in his Ferret Fantasy catalogue) it was rare to find copies signed by the editor/publisher!

George managed to get the better of me on a number of subsequent occasions, such as when I acquired his wonderful *Spectrum of Fantasy* volumes by trading Tartarus Press books of a much higher retail value. (To be fair, his reference books are still a delight, and I have completely forgotten which books he had in exchange.) I always grumbled, but usually admired the way he would end up with the better part of any deal.

One reason I kept in touch with George, and occasionally bought from him, was his suggestion that he had several Machen books I might like, although these never quite seemed to materialise.

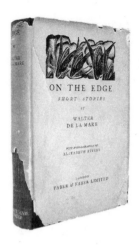

19

On the Edge

WALTER DE LA MARE

Faber and Faber, 1930

One bookshop that has been in operation for ever, as far as I am concerned, is Camilla's in Eastbourne. I remember that thirty-five years ago there were piles of books ascending towards the tall ceiling in the vast main room, and I thought at the time they could never grow any taller. Nor did I think that the heaps of books on the floor in the basement could proliferate any further. However, year after year the stock has increased inexorably. I love the shop, but more than half the books inside are inaccessible.

Up the stairs to the first floor, there have always been shelves of collectable fiction, and I have invariably unearthed some minor treasures there. I remember buying a first edition of *On the Edge* by Walter de la Mare in about 1990, having read the marvellous 'Seaton's Aunt' in one of my cheap paperback anthologies. 'Seaton's Aunt' (1921) is a wonderfully creepy short story, not least because the reader doesn't quite know what to believe by the end. I've reread it several times over the years and it never fails to unsettle. Amongst aficionados of ghost stories de la Mare is considered one of the 'golden age' authors of such tales, but if he is popularly remembered today it is as a poet, and for his work for children, such as 'The Listeners'.

On the Edge still had the remains of a shabby jacket clinging to it and the cloth was faded and marked, but I loved the soft, laid paper inside. I remember reading the first story, 'A Recluse', and enjoying the fact that it was another ghost story that left questions unanswered. In a Twayne study of de la Mare, Doris Ross McCrosson wrote:

His preoccupation with good and evil puts him on a level with Hawthorne and Conrad; his mastery of suspense and terror is equal to Poe's; the subtlety of his characterisations occasionally rivals James's. And the range of his portrayals is impressive: children, old maids, the demented, old idealists and young pessimists, artists, businessmen, dandys, young women in love – all of whom share in the mysterious and sometimes maddening business called living.

I would add that de la Mare's hauntings are rarely conventional, and are very often personal and melancholy. There is usually a psychological element, and absence and loss are at the heart of many of them.

I remember reading a further story in *On the Edge* (it would probably have been the next, 'Willows') and although I enjoyed it, I was disappointed it was not ghostly. I read another couple of stories at random and was likewise let down to find them

108

'straight' stories, although there was always a palpable atmosphere to them. I appreciated 'Crewe' (another classic ghostly tale), but it was some time later, perhaps a few years, before I got round to reading 'The Green Room'. For some reason I had assumed that this was also non-ghostly, but it is calculated to be perfect for a reader like me – it is a tale of the supernatural set in a bookshop. A young man is invited into the private annexe that exists in all bookshops, and here he discovers a volume of poems in manuscript and glimpses the ghost of its author.

After 'The Green Room' I revisited the rest of the volume, and realised that I shouldn't have allowed myself to be limited to de la Mare's ghost stories; his other stories are of a comparable high quality and atmosphere. His whole oeuvre is worth reading.

Shortly after Rosalie and I moved to Sussex in the 1990s and began haunting Brighton's bookshops together, a new business appeared at 31 Trafalgar Street: Grimoire Bookshop. This was the joint enterprise of Catherine Walton (who had previously been selling books in Brighton) and Brian Banks, a London book dealer who continued to trade as Déjà vu Books.

The Grimoire Bookshop was a treasure cave of decadent and occult books, but, memorably, the shop was also full of occult artefacts, antiques, tribal art and curios. I was tempted by the skulls, and it may have been here that I bought my Aleister Crowley Thoth tarot pack. There were some very strange customers who were, no doubt, associated with the nearby Temple of Psychic Youth. I never saw Genesis P-Orridge in the shop, although he was a regular customer, especially interested in occult items and Crowleyania.

I remember we bought antiques at Grimoire, but the only book I remember buying was Crowley's *The Stratagem*, published by the Temple Press. The trouble is that Grimoire is a bookshop about which I really remember the books I *didn't* buy. My chief regret was not being able to afford a signed copy of Arthur Machen's *The Hill of Dreams*. I was allowed to leaf through the book in an office upstairs, shared with pigeons, where the Déjà vu catalogues were compiled. The book was an odd edition, issued in 1923 by Martin Secker in a run of only 150 signed copies, on blue paper. There is a good reason why books are rarely printed on such paper – it is not easy on the eye – but I always regretted not buying it.

I can't help thinking that Grimoire is one of those shops which it would be wonderful to visit in a time machine. Their books by Austin Osman Spare, and even a painting by the artist, were not cheap in the 1990s, but would cost a small fortune now.

Grimoire was a shop about which wonderful rumours persisted long after it suddenly closed. Catherine was said to have had for sale Crowley's dagger, a human mummy, and sold an original handwritten alchemical manuscript to a hermetic museum in Amsterdam. Catherine would put a curse on the door if something significant was stolen, and the story was that the item would be 'magically' returned through the letterbox. Driff, though, was annoyed that the shop took legal measures to get him to pay a bill rather than settle for turning him into a frog. Presumably it was not worth resorting to magic when the law was equally effective. Other stories I've heard suggest that Catherine had the carved sign from a scold's ducking stool in her collection at home, and a mummified Horus hawk. I've since been assured that these stories are true.

Examples of the catalogues produced by Brian and Catherine are now held in the Museum of Witchcraft and Magic in Boscastle, Cornwall. I must still have my copies somewhere, but I haven't dug them out because I am bound to come across the listing for that blue-paper edition of *The Hill of Dreams*.

I have reread *The Hill of Dreams* several times over the years. Oddly, it was only when I moved back to the countryside that I fully appreciated the episodes set in the city. Machen's description of the streets and their potential for mystery suddenly made sense. London, for Machen, was just as full of possibilities for the strange and marvellous as the countryside.

On later visits to Caerleon and its environs I have discovered, with friends, the true model for the Hill of Dreams — Lodge Hill, above Caerleon. The episode in the novel when Lucian finds himself inside the old hill fort on a hot summer day fits the location perfectly. With its steep banks and ditches, impenetrable thickets and memorable nettles, Lodge Hill is as atmospheric in winter (when the branches reach, black and writhing, into a leaden sky), as it is in summer, when Lucian Taylor visits it and falls into a reverie:

Within the fort it was all dusky and cool and hollow; it was as if one stood at the bottom of a great cup. Within, the wall seemed higher than without, and the ring of oaks curved up like a dark green vault. There were nettles growing thick and rank in the foss; they looked different from

the common nettles in the lanes, and Lucian, letting his
hand touch a leaf by accident, felt the sting burn like fire.

Lucian's dream of Caerleon in its heyday is unsurpassed in
imaginative literature, especially in his evocation of a Roman
tavern:

> The walls of the tavern were covered with pictures painted
> in violent hues; blues and reds and greens jarring against
> one another and lighting up the gloom of the place. The
> stone benches were always crowded, the sunlight came in
> through the door in a long bright beam, casting a dancing
> shadow of vine leaves on the further wall. There a painter
> had made a joyous figure of the young Bacchus driving
> the leopards before him with his ivy-staff, and the quiv-
> ering shadow seemed a part of the picture. The room was
> cool and dark and cavernous, but the scent and heat of
> the summer gushed in through the open door. There was
> ever a full sound, with noise and vehemence, there, and
> the rolling music of the Latin tongue never ceased.

The Hill of Dreams has become something of a touchstone for
me. When I occasionally find somebody else who has read
it, I admit I judge them on their reaction to the book. What
I find is that readers view *The Hill of Dreams* in different ways,
depending on their own experiences of life. If they have only
read it once, it strikes me as entirely reasonable if they do not
appreciate its depth – various aspects of this book have only
been revealed to me by reading it again and again.

*   *   *

I first heard about Frederick Rolfe at the Aylesford Conference at Wistaston Hall, Crewe, in 1994. I attended with Mark Valentine, Roger Dobson and Dr Gail-Nina Anderson, a small group of relatively young people brought in to bolster the dwindling number of original, elderly members. The event was a strange survival of a once very popular residential literary, right-wing, Catholic weekend. At my first meeting I was introduced to the humourless King Leo of Redonda, the curiously named Wheatley Blench, David Ashton (engaged in writing a thesis on pop music, despite never having heard of The Beatles or The Rolling Stones) and Devendra Varma. The latter gave a memorable lecture on the women in Bram Stoker's *Dracula*, but his faculties were failing and he sadly confused fact and fantasy, causing his small audience to exchange profound frowns with each other for over an hour.

Brocard Sewell was the originator of the Aylesford Conferences, and their only true survivor. He had once worked with Eric Gill at the Ditchling Press, and when I gave him a copy of my first hardback publication, Machen's *Ritual and Other Stories*, he noted the typeface I had used: 'Times New Roman?' He then added, 'An admirable choice for newspapers, but it was never intended for books. Do not use it again.' I didn't.

At that meeting Frederick Rolfe was discussed at some length, and he was made to sound fascinating. I immediately scoured the second-hand bookshops for him and found *Hadrian the Seventh*. After the excellent opening chapter, I became bored. I unearthed the *Toto* stories, but they didn't appeal, and I tried several of his other books, *Nicholas Crabbe, Don Tarquinio* and *Don Renato*. All appeared to me, in their different ways, unreadable. However ...

113

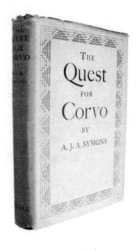

20

The Quest for Corvo

A. J. A. SYMONS

Cassell, 1934

It was David Jarman in the Disjecta bookshop, Pipe Passage, Lewes who recommended A. J. A. Symons's incomparable *The Quest for Corvo*. The recommendation was heartily endorsed by the man who ran the private library upstairs (which I could not afford to join).

The Quest for Corvo is a biography of Frederick Rolfe told obliquely through Symons's attempts to discover the details of the author's life, and it is rightly considered a twentieth-century classic. In his radical approach to Rolfe/Corvo, Symons altered the course of literary biography. He declared that the purpose of biography was 'not to record but to reveal', and in this he succeeded admirably. Symons's primary aim was to tell how he came across the facts of Rolfe's life, and we learn about Rolfe almost incidentally. Several critics have noted that by subordinating his subject to the quest itself, Symons does Rolfe a disservice. Those same critics have pointed out that Symons also makes the facts of the quest secondary to his desire to tell an entertaining story, and though this may be true, it is to forget that the details of Rolfe's life would be almost completely unknown without Symons's ability to report so compellingly on how he unearthed them. Symons single-handedly created the 'Corvo Cult', resulting in the more conventional biographies by Weeks and Benkovitz, the publication and republication of a great deal of Corviana, and the skyward spiral in prices for rare and collectable material by and about Rolfe.

Symons's radical approach in *The Quest for Corvo* has given ammunition to Rolfe sympathisers and apologists. Even Brocard Sewell, editor of *New Quests for Corvo*, admitted the tendency of admirers to 'sentimentalise' their subject. The problem is that Rolfe was a man of many admirable qualities, including unbounded enthusiasm, determination and energy. He was clever and could be charming company. And when he was not attempting to be archaic, he had the ability to write a very readable sentence. And it is always romantically appealing when an author is a true outsider and can reasonably be considered an underdog. Added to all of this, he was homosexual at a time when it was a very serious crime. He also had a genuine desire to be a priest, but was thwarted by the authorities. He was often hard done by and abused, and misfortune can have an heroic aspect, no matter that he brought most of his troubles down upon his own head.

Rolfe appears to have had an impressive 'sense of entitlement', and a vindictive streak that could be so passionate and unreasonable and inventive that it was almost superhuman. Time after time Rolfe was aided, often very generously, by friends and strangers through their genuine liking for the man, only for him to exploit that friendship and generosity, twist it, misrepresent it and viciously attack those who had only ever wanted to help him. His supporters R. H. Benson and C. H. C. Pirie-Gordon were inevitably turned into the Reverend Bobugo Bonson and Peary-Buthlaw, respectively, in Rolfe's fiction, but the Baron often went beyond mere name-calling. When he became seriously exasperated by Benson and Pirie-Gordon, he announced his intention to produce a pornographic work with R. H. B. on the title page and the Pirie-Gordon coat of arms on the cover. He couldn't help but get himself into trouble: when he stayed with the van Somerens in Venice, being given, gratis, his own apartment in the vast Palazzo Corner Mocenigo, he used the time to 'pitilessly lampoon' his hosts' friends with 'perverse and brilliant ingenuity', writing a book that was 'rancid with libel'.

In fact, so much of Rolfe's time, energy, ingenuity and resources went into making enemies, and exacting colourful revenge, that vituperation can be reasonably considered to have been his greatest talent and crowning achievement . . . all of which makes, in the hands of A. J. A. Symons, a wonderfully vital biography.

*　　*　　*

A book dealer I got to know in Sussex who exemplified a delightfully old-fashioned attitude towards bookselling was Tim Scott. I met him at a book fair and he phoned me later, saying that he had a couple of Machen first editions I might like. I arranged to meet him at his home in Lewes, where I was invited into a room best described as a 'parlour', where tea was served (as at The Lilies) in china cups, and we sat around talking about books and authors for half an hour. When I reminded him that he might have some Machen for me, he brought out first editions of *Far Off Things* (1922) and *Things Near and Far* (1923). As though it pained him, he suggested a price, and I handed over the cash. Once this transaction was over he relaxed again.

One of the subjects we discussed was the Bloomsbury Group, about which I knew very little and he a great deal. I admitted to him that a year or so earlier I had walked towards the village of Kingston, where a friend of Sylvia Townsend Warner, Trekkie Parsons, lived. She was the wife of Ian Parsons, who had been Warner's publisher. That day I walked over the Downs was very hot (I still remember the skylarks), and I was delighted to meet Trekkie (she was working in her garden). She invited me inside for refreshments, and we talked about her friendship with Warner. At some point she had mentioned the Bloomsbury artists, and I was very disparaging of them in a high-handed, completely ignorant way. It was after I had said my piece that I noticed, all around her walls, the kind of paintings that I had just been dismissing as 'colourful daubs'. Not only was Trekkie on the edge of the Bloomsbury Group and had a great deal many pictures by their artists, but she, too, painted, and in the same style.

It was not long after I had admitted my mistake to Tim Scott that he called me again, mentioning, vaguely, that he had a book that might interest me. This time he brought it out as soon as I arrived, before the tea had even brewed. It was Sylvia Townsend Warner's *The Portrait of a Tortoise*, published by Chatto & Windus in 1946. It was a first edition with a letter tipped in from Warner to Ian Parsons, her publisher, thanking him for the book. Apparently Tim and Trekkie had discussed my faux pas about the Bloomsbury artists, which she had thought hilarious. She had passed the book on to Tim in the hope that I might appreciate it.

21

The
Unspeakable
Skipton

PAMELA HANSFORD
JOHNSON

Macmillan, 1959

It was in the Disjecta bookshop that David Jarman later offered me a copy of *The Unspeakable Skipton*, claiming that it was a remarkably accurate portrait of a narcissist. Pamela Hansford Johnson makes it clear that she had Frederick Rolfe in mind, and that such characters are not just painfully curious but are to be pitied – as long as they can be kept at a distance.

In this quiet masterpiece of a novel, Hansford Johnson tells the story of an English author living in poverty in Bruges. Daniel Skipton has previously had some commercial success, but is eternally frustrated that nobody else shares his very high opinion of his writing. He recognises that he is capable of being hateful and vindictive, but in his own eyes this is only ever with good, justifiable reason. He survives in Bruges by accepting advances from his publisher (despite knowing that his latest book will never be accepted) and sponging off a distant relative, while taking advantage of his landlady and her daughter. Skipton is entirely predatory, swindling tourists in league with an unscrupulous antiques dealer, and even making a little money acting as a pimp.

Skipton's only real joy in life is writing, but there is no consideration of story or plot in his latest work – it is simply a vehicle for settling old scores and redressing perceived wrongs in language which he agonises over and polishes to perfection. When he comes up against an equally narcissistic but more successful author, Dorothy, he anticipates that at a public lecture she will be obliged to praise his work. The reader knows, long before Skipton, that this will never happen, but Pamela Hansford Johnson describes his self-delusion so skilfully that the reader almost sympathises with him. Skipton is entirely responsible for his own situation, but he can do nothing about it. He is motivated by an overinflated belief in his talent and a need to correct perceived injustices, but simple survival has also become a factor, so that when he moves into the orbit of another swindler, it is difficult to decide which of them, if either, deserves to triumph.

*   *   *

By this time I had become a much more active member of the Arthur Machen Society, editing an edition of the journal and helping guest editors with theirs. I even looked after Mr and Mrs X's house for a month, keeping an eye on their business while they were away. It was a good excuse to spend some time going through the Machen collection at Newport Reference Library (I produced a catalogue for them of their collection), as well as spending time in the bookshops of nearby Hay-on-Wye.

I suggested to Mrs X that I would organise a pub crawl in London following a forthcoming Saturday afternoon meeting for Society members in Amersham. Several people expressed an interest in gathering first at the Cheshire Cheese, but over the weeks leading up to it, one by one they fell away with this or that legitimate excuse, so that I went into London from Amersham sure that I would be on my own. I nursed a pint of Guinness for half an hour, and just as I was about to leave a tall, balding man appeared and unerringly made for my table.

'Mr Russell,' he intoned. 'I . . . am Gerald Suster.'

We shook hands and I offered to buy him a pint, which he accepted.

'No doubt you have heard of me,' he said, and I made some non-committal comment about not being privy to the details of Society membership.

'I am the author of *The Devil's Maze*,' he said grandly. When I looked blank he suggested that I might have heard of *The Elect*? The next title he tried was *The Scar*, and then, still hopeful, *The Offering*?

When I failed to recognise any of his fiction he tried again with his non-fiction.

'*Hitler and the Age of Horus*? *John Dee: Essential Readings*? *Hitler: Black Magician*? *The Legacy of the Beast*?'

I chose a title at random, claiming that I had seen it, and perhaps even owned a copy. I don't believe I would have claimed to have read it. I think I must have opted for *The Legacy of the Beast*, because he then discoursed upon 'The Beast 666' on the assumption that I knew all about Aleister Crowley and his works. I am certain that I would have been able to nod at appropriate moments, and must have expressed periodic interest in, or surprise at, his revelations.

I met Gerald Suster again a year later on another London pub crawl I organised, which was rather better attended. I believe that Roger Dobson and Mark Samuels were there. Gerald brought along his wife, Michaela. This time he was a rather more considerate companion, but he insisted on derailing our arrangements by taking us to The Princess Louise in Holborn (which was, and is, a very fine pub), and then on to some spit-and-sawdust establishment somewhere beyond Shoreditch. It had hard benches covered in red linoleum and tin-topped tables, and he and Michaela were the only ones to appreciate its charms. I remember that it was a very long walk to the nearest Tube station.

On this second pub crawl, others must have been given a chance to speak, because Gerald discovered I was a publisher. (I had published articles by both Roger and Mark, and these might have been discussed.) Within days a mass of typescript arrived in the post with a covering letter from Gerald explaining that he would be happy for me to publish his collection of short stories. We had only to come to a suitable financial arrangement.

I must admit that I began reading with some enthusiasm. If Gerald really was the great writer he claimed, and as notorious as he said (he had been defamed by the *News of the World* and suggested that he had received vast damages), a collection of his stories ought to sell well. The first story was a riff on M. P. Shiel's 'Xélucha', but the comparison was not to Gerald's credit. I am not sure why he smuggled the sport of boxing into the tale, but all the stories that followed were boxing-themed and homoerotic.

I don't think that I was always tactful in my youth, and I had definite views on literature, but there was no need to say anything other than that the stories were unlikely to appeal to Tartarus Press customers. I was actually quite annoyed that he had tried to pass off such second-rate work on me.

The result of the rejection was our receipt of a postcard with a magic curse written on the back. I wish I had kept it, but Rosalie was unimpressed by me tucking it inside my copy of Gerald's *The God Game* as a souvenir. Not that she believed it had any power (far from it), but she was less than overwhelmed by the sentiment, and threw it in the bin.

22

The Cry
of a Gull

ALYSE GREGORY

The Ark Press, 1973

I first read *The Cry of a Gull* in 1995 when Rosalie and I stayed
at Janet Machen's holiday cottage, Chydyok, near East Chaldon
in Dorset. What caught my eye on the bookshelf was the unu-
sually tall format of the book, and I was intrigued by the light
blue paper on which it was printed. The book offered extracts
from Alyse Gregory's diaries over a period of twenty-five years,
many of them written at Chydyok. It was both compelling and
heart-rending, as the first half of the book tells of how her
husband, Llewelyn Powys, would leave Chydyok to tramp over
the Downs to nearby White Nothe, where he was conducting
an affair with another writer, Gamel Woolsey. This was done
with Alyse's full knowledge:

> June 11 [1931]: Tomorrow morning he is to meet her on
> the downs.

124

It seemed almost unbearably painful – how could Llewelyn have been so cruel to his wife? On rereading it years later my reaction was more ambivalent – Alyse may have worshipped her husband, but did she have to collude with his infidelity so uncomplainingly?

> February 20, 1932: Llewelyn went walking with Gerald Brenan and I stayed and talked with Gamel. There was between Gamel and me so delicate an understanding. We are so much alike in so many ways, my heart went out to her and I knew that she could harbour no real unkindness. She has a curious innocence. She is both wise and innocent. I was happy that I could love her, that I could feel my old desire to protect her.

That Alyse loved Llewelyn profoundly is beyond doubt – so much so that she made excuses for him:

> April 5, 1932: When Llewelyn kissed me this morning telling me that he loved me 'Oh, so deeply', I knew that it was because he was going over there. It is always thus. And yet he cannot help it.

Llewelyn Powys died on 2 December 1939, and the second half of the book chronicles Alyse Gregory's life alone. She wrote on 23 December:

> I sit in my little attic room from where I used to look out at Llewelyn in his garden house. My cat, full of its secret life, follows me about in the deserted rooms.

It was all the more powerful reading these lines while in Alyse's own room under the roof at Chydyok, which resembles an upturned boat.

On New Year's Day, 1941 she wrote of the ravages of war 'and the loss of Llewelyn still a constant pain in my heart'. Three years later:

> February 14, 1944: This afternoon I heard the first spring notes of the birds. It made me cry, and Llewelyn has never in all this time left my heart, nor ever will until I am dead as earth.

Another four years later she writes:

> August 13 [1948]: Llewelyn's birthday – very cold and rainy, not his weather. Still I dream – when I do dream of him – unhappy dreams, of him and Gamel.

The Afterword by Michael Adam to the Chydyok copy of *The Cry of a Gull* was heavily annotated in Janet Machen's unmistakable firm handwriting. Janet's comments (mainly corrections of fact, although one just states: 'Rubbish!') amused me so much that when I bought my own copy of the book from Julian Nangle, I transferred them into it. I also bought myself a copy of Llewelyn Powys's *Skin for Skin*, which I had also read at Chydyok, because no matter what I thought of the author as a person, his essays are superb.

I am pleased to report that the ghosts of Alyse and Llewelyn were exorcised by the boisterous Machen family, who had taken over Chydyok and made it their own. There was a reverence for those who had come before them, but it was neither a museum nor a shrine. It is sad to relate that in recent years the Machen family have lost the lease of the cottage. It has since been 'renovated'.

I first discussed forming a Sylvia Townsend Warner Society with Janet Machen in 1993. I am not sure if the idea was mine or hers. Janet was Sylvia's cousin, and she hoped that a literary society could be established similar to the one devoted to her father. The Machen Society continued to be convivial and energetic, and the membership was keenly promoting Machen's writings. A Sylvia Townsend Warner Society could have a similar regular journal and newsletter, hold events, readings, etc. As with the Arthur Machen Society, Janet would be Patron.

I was still collecting Sylvia Townsend Warner's books and researching my *Bibliography* – in those pre-internet days, corresponding with book dealers through the post and visiting libraries. I had a number of collecting coups, the most important of which was buying the original ending of *Lolly Willowes* (1926). The bookseller Judith Stinton discovered this in the possession of one of the author's near neighbours, scribbled in Warner's distinctive handwriting in biro on notepaper.

The only problem I encountered was accessing the Sylvia Townsend Warner collection, then housed in Dorchester Museum by the Dorset Natural History and Archaeological Society. Admission was controlled by Warner's literary executor, whom I shall call Ms Y, who steadfastly refused to grant most applicants permission to visit. This caused frustration not only for researchers, but also for the director of the Dorset Natural History and Archaeological Society.

After much negotiation, a back-door entrance was eventually contrived.

Rosalie was also enthusiastic about founding an STW Society, and together we sent out speculative letters to various interested parties. These included Ms Y, several of Sylvia's old friends (contact details provided by Janet), and various academics and enthusiasts we knew would be interested. This letter excitedly proposed that the Society would promote the wider publication of Sylvia Townsend Warner's writings because, at the time, there was *nothing* by her in print, despite Virago having the rights to publish.

The enraged reply I received from the literary estate made it very clear that our venture would not have their approval. We withdrew our plans, because a Society without the support of the estate would not have been viable. But Janet would not be dissuaded. She was experienced enough to take her time and play a long game.

Flower Phantoms

RONALD FRASER

Cape, 1926

Mark Valentine recommended the books of Ronald Fraser, and in the 1990s they seemed to cluster on the shelves of every bookshop and could be bought in the Cape first editions for very little money. One that I read had an interesting (H. G. Wellsian) conceit at its heart: *The Flying Draper* (1931) was about a man who learns how to fly unaided by any kind of technology. It is hard not to damn Fraser's books with what sounds like faint praise – they are good novels, but there is also a temptation to describe them as 'good *little* novels', which is unjust. They are very well written, but quietly undemonstrative. I have three more of his books on my shelves, but I failed to finish two of them because other books clamoured to be read in their place, and I didn't feel the need to return.

However, one book by Fraser does strike me as worth reading, revisiting and recommending – *Flower Phantoms*. This, I know, is Mark's favourite, and I was delighted to come across my copy in the Disjecta bookshop not long after Mark mentioned it to me. I felt a little guilty when he said that his own copy, unlike the one I had just bought, didn't have a dust jacket. But then, in a case of serendipity (probably because I was now aware of what it looked like), I came across another copy in a jacket only a few hundred yards away in Bow Windows Bookshop. It was only right to return the favour of Mark's recommendation by passing on the duplicate to him. The jacket is a nice one, although the woodcut artist was unable to delineate the nude figure with any skill.

Flower Phantoms tells of a young botanical student, Judy, working at Kew Gardens. Her home life is rather constricted, but amongst the plants her imagination and insight reveal a secret dimension to the rich earth- and flower-scented world of orchids, water lilies and ferns. It is a story of a fervent spiritual and erotic awakening that is vivid and passionate, while sensitively written. It is heady stuff – especially when she discovers romantic affinities with a giant orchid. The pleasant young man to whom she is engaged cannot compare favourably with her hothouse encounters and experiences.

The *Times Literary Supplement* commented at the time,

> The book abounds in glowing experiences of a world of colour and sensation, minutely imagined . . . The description of dawn at Kew Gardens is so lovely that the reader will be tempted to endanger his respectability by emulating Judy and climbing the wall.

The incomparable critic E. F. Bleiler later wrote that the novel was 'Told with delicate imagery and fine perceptions, a minor rococoism of art deco literature.'

But I will leave the last word to Mark Valentine, who resurrected the book with an American small press, Valancourt, in 2013:

There is a chaste sensuality in Fraser's writing, and a spiritual ardour which is often the equal of the most successful passages in Machen or Blackwood.

*   *   *

As my reading widened over time, I began to collect books by various authors. I had my own 'wants' list, but I also started to collect bibliographies of various authors I liked, very often photocopied from the pages of the *Book and Magazine Collector*. I bought Joseph Connelly's *Collecting Modern First Editions* and *Breese's Guide to Modern First Editions*, both of which were useful, but what I really wanted was a paperback of bibliographies with up-to-date values that would fit in my pocket. As such a book did not exist, I was spurred on to compile and publish my first *Guide to First Edition Prices* (1997), which eventually went through eight editions. I embarked upon the first with a great deal of enthusiasm, culling information from a wide variety of sources and sending off for, and receiving, catalogues from very many book dealers around the country and in the USA. Until the very last issue (2010), the *Guides* were a great success, but rechecking the prices every time, with a pressure to add more and more books and authors, became a deadly chore, even with specialist dealers and collectors to help me (collating information from a wide variety of correspondents was a full-time job). The last issue contained

131

50,000 sought-after books by 720 authors; the *Guides* ended because sales declined with the growth of the internet. Book collectors reasoned that they could find the same information online for free.

The Oscar Wilde comment about the man who 'knows the price of everything and the value of nothing' was often made by critics. I recall the *Times Literary Supplement*'s NB Column frequently claiming that my suggested values were too low and calling me 'Parsimonious Russell'. I prided myself on always rechecking prices for each edition, so complaints stung, especially when the continuous revaluations removed the original enjoyment of compiling the *Guide*. When I visited bookshops I often mentioned my book (without revealing who I was), only for the owner to tell me that they didn't need to buy any guides. Very often I knew they had bought a copy from me direct, just a few weeks before.

I can't help thinking that the satisfaction in collecting the information on titles, publishers, dates of publication, and so on, was similar to the enjoyment I had once found in collecting tea cards and creating sets to fill albums. For a decade, the *Guides* subsidised Tartarus Press, allowing me to publish and stay at home looking after our son, Tim, who was born in 1995.

A Little
Treachery

PHYLLIS PAUL

Norton, 1962

Dr Glen Cavaliero devoted seven pages of his book *The Supernatural and English Fiction* to the work of Phyllis Paul (1903–1973), piquing the interest of various readers looking for recommendations for underappreciated writers. It was not the first time he had praised her work, but it was where many collectors first heard of her. They hoovered up the few books available on the second-hand market and prices skyrocketed.

In 1996, Glen was the guest speaker at the annual dinner of the Arthur Machen Society. He admitted to me that his book had really been an excuse to write about Paul, whose work had been introduced to him by Phyllis Playter, the wife of John Cowper Powys. It is interesting how literary connections are made for readers.

Phyllis Paul wrote twelve novels, of which eleven were published and one is lost. In a later article for *Wormwood*, Glen wrote: 'Phyllis Paul was that rare creature, a puritan with a passionate and colourful imagination.' He claimed that 'running through all her novels is an undercurrent of the supernatural: her concern is not so much with psychological issues as with those of the spirit.'

Perhaps the most accessible of her novels, and the easiest obtained, is *Twice Lost* (published in 1960, and reprinted in the USA as a mass-market paperback in 1966). It is about a young girl, Vivian, who has disappeared but who seems to return fifteen years later, prompting a great deal of suspicion as to whether she is who she claims to be. There are different potential explanations for the events in the book, but the story never comes fully to life. I would suggest that Paul's most readable novel is *A Cage for the Nightingale* (1957), a dark mystery of some sophistication. Most of her other novels have not resonated with me, or have been unobtainable, but the one with the longest legacy in my memory is *A Little Treachery*. I am including it here although it is, perhaps, the most miserable book I have ever read.

A Little Treachery concerns two sisters, Catherine and Clem Hare, who are described as being infected by a prolonged 'close proximity' to their mother's madness. They are persuaded to buy a mean and unsuitable old cottage – damp because it is built into a hillside, and hard up against a main road, so it vibrates with the passing traffic. Soon after they move in, Clem follows in her mother's footsteps and is incarcerated. Catherine is forced to take in a lodger, the unconventional Emmy Rivers, and a troubled young boy, the son of the man who persuaded Clem and her sister to take the house in the first place. Both Catherine and the boy become dependent on Emmy, who then abandons them. The atmosphere of misery in their horrible dwelling is palpable, and matters become worse . . .

If the book is memorably gloomy, it doesn't really help to know that Glen Cavaliero was convinced *A Little Treachery* was semi-autobiographical. Little is known about Phyllis Paul's life, but it is understood that her own sister suffered a mental breakdown. Most of Paul's books have mental illness and its effects on others in the background, although I came away from *A Little Treachery* with a horror not of Catherine Hare's family situation so much as revulsion at the soul-destroying and gloomy house and garden where the story is set. It is almost as though it is the poisoned atmosphere of the immediate physical surrounding that destroys any chance of happiness for the characters. Phyllis Paul was a powerful writer, but not a particularly happy one.

*   *   *

There are times when you can find yourself embroiled in unexpected battles, even in literary societies where so little might appear to be at stake. The Arthur Machen Society was an important part of my life for a number of years, but, as time progressed, publications became less regular, the organised events became less bohemian and more rarefied and expensive, and only tangentially Machenian. When I explained this problem to Mrs X she made me Members' Representative, but this only meant that I received complaints that I then had to pass on to her.

Matters came to a head in September 1996 when a member from Tunbridge Wells phoned to ask why he'd had a subscription reminder when he had received no journals or newsletters in the previous year. When I passed this complaint on to Mrs X, her reaction was such that I could only share Mr Talbot's concerns. She could not explain how the subscriptions had been spent, and when I suggested that this was an unsatis-factory situation, she launched an unpleasant personal attack upon me. I was confused and hurt, and I could see no option but to resign. I had lost a good friend, but what upset me most was the reduced opportunity to see so many other friends who were, by now, very important to me.

25

Stenbock, Yeats and the Nineties

JOHN ADLARD

Cecil Woolf, 1969

I don't know from whom I first heard of Count Stenbock, some time in the 1990s. It may have been Mark Valentine and Roger Dobson, although it was just as likely to have been the musician David Tibet. Stenbock's books, at that period, were fabulously rare and unobtainable, and the few who had heard of him would recall W. B. Yeats's oft-quoted description of him as a 'scholar, connoisseur, drunkard, poet, pervert, most charming of men'. John Adlard's biography of Stenbock, which was very difficult to obtain (or so I thought – I paid quite a lot for my copy), revealed that his subject was an 1890s decadent who knew Oscar Wilde, took industrial quantities of drugs, kept a menagerie and was accompanied by a life-size human doll that he considered his son and heir. It helped the Stenbock myth that his very few books had wonderfully evocative titles: *Love, Sleep & Dreams* (1881); *Myrtle, Rue and Cypress* (1883); *The Shadow of Death* (1893); *Studies of Death* (1894). It almost didn't matter how good his writing was because one was never

137

likely to read it. (He received, in his time, very few, usually lukewarm, reviews.)

As an antidote to my unhappiness at having to resign from the Arthur Machen Society, and my inability to start a Sylvia Townsend Warner Society, I decided to form the Stenbock Society, which was not entirely a spoof – we did issue one publication, bound with a peacock's feather. To make the running of the Stenbock Society as easy as possible I decided to limit the membership, arbitrarily, to eleven. These were: myself, Rosalie, our son Tim, Mark Valentine, Roger Dobson, David Tibet, John Balance, Rhys Hughes, Timothy d'Arch Smith and the ghost of John Adlard. Mark Samuels was invited, although I can't remember if he agreed to join. I later allowed a couple of additional members, including the poet Jeremy Reed, assuming that Rosalie, Tim and I had a joint family membership. So that nobody would ask what we did with the subscription money, I decided there would be no membership fee.

I was talking to the journalist Byron Rogers about Machen and the future of the Society (which appeared moribund at that point) when he told me he had just attended the annual meeting of the Alliance of Literary Societies, expecting the Machenians to have been there. He had been impressed that the Beddoes Society attended none of the programmed events because they never left the pub, and I, in a game of literary one-upmanship, pointed out that the Stenbock Society hadn't even bothered to attend, due to ennui. He dutifully wrote about the Stenbockians in a long article in the *Telegraph* magazine.

I then discovered that John Adlard's *Stenbock, Yeats and the Nineties* was still in print, available at the cover price direct from the publisher. Cecil Woolf admitted that he still had one box remaining; Tibet and I jointly bought it and gave copies as gifts to members of the Stenbock Society and to others we hoped would be sympathetic.

David Tibet has been Stenbock's real champion. He not only tracked down copies of the author's super-rare first editions, but in 1996 he published a facsimile reprint of *Studies of Death* under his Durtro imprint. This edition was limited to 300 copies, and is now expensive and collectable itself. Other Durtro editions of Stenbock's work appeared as Tibet evangelised, reprinting rare publications and unearthing new material. Tibet's knowledge of the author convinced him that his subject was not only a very colourful literary curiosity, but an interesting and talented writer. Tibet admits that Stenbock will never be accepted by the mainstream, or considered one of the 'greats', but other publishers have been inspired to publish more mass-market editions of Stenbock's poetry, prose and plays. These have all built on Tibet's work (not always acknowledging it), and for a very modest outlay it is now possible to fully evaluate Stenbock. He remains an archetypal tragic Decadent, albeit a nuanced one, and his work is far better and more interesting than had been expected by many previously frustrated would-be readers.

What the world needs, however, is a new biography of Stenbock (and Tibet ought to be the author). In the meantime, John Adlard's *Stenbock, Yeats and the Nineties* is a great read and, dare I suggest, more interesting than anything Stenbock wrote himself.

Unknown to me, after my resignation from the Machen Society Mrs X was receiving other complaints. She published a new edition of the journal (which made a pointed attack on me). She announced a number of new events, including a Roman Catholic Mass in memory of Machen (he was an Anglican), an evening of John Ireland's music, which seemed more for the benefit of the Ireland Society, and an afternoon cream tea with the Gwent Youth Orchestra. Iain Smith and other Northern members began organising their own regular meet-ups outside the official Society, forming the Ancient Order of Banwick, offering more affordable, relaxed and convivial meetings.

And then, unexpectedly, Mrs X sent a fax asking me to take over the running of the Society. After some thought I agreed, on the understanding that we must have an elected committee to make decisions, with a treasurer and annual accounts. It would also have to be understood that the majority of the subscription income would be spent on regular publications for the membership. Although Mrs X agreed, once we were back on an even keel, solvent and publishing regularly, she announced she didn't like the direction we were moving in and insisted on taking back control. The resulting battle became very personal, not least because Mrs X would not accept that a committee was making decisions. That committee was made up of active members, including Jon Preece, Godfrey Brangham, Mark Valentine and Roger Dobson. We were backed by Janet Machen and many other members of long standing, but still Mrs X insisted on an unseemly battle. The only way to end the hostility was to pass the Society back to Mrs X, under whose control it withered and died. In its place was founded the Friends of Arthur Machen, which continues to thrive.

26

The Haunted Woman

DAVID LINDSAY

Methuen 1922. My copy: Gollancz, 1947

When David Lindsay is remembered at all, it is usually for his very early science fiction fantasy *A Voyage to Arcturus* (1920), a novel in which an adventurer, Maskull, travels to Tormance, an imaginary planet orbiting Arcturus, and moves through various surreal landscapes representing different philosophical systems and states of mind. It has some affinities with *Gulliver's Travels*, and to modern sensibilities it reads more like fantasy than science fiction. (As do, for example, Edgar Rice Burroughs's *John Carter of Mars* books from just a decade before *Arcturus*.) Sales of the first edition of *Arcturus* were poor, but over the years it has been regularly reprinted and revived. It was apparently an influence on C. S. Lewis, who recommended it to J. R. R. Tolkien. Writers such as Clive Barker, Michael Moorcock and Philip Pullman have all praised it.

Less well known is another Lindsay novel, *The Haunted Woman*. Lindsay set out to write something more commercial and conventional after *Arcturus*, although sales of *The Haunted Woman* were just as poor. It is more accessible, and, arguably, every bit as interesting. It tells of Isbel Loment, who is engaged to a very dull and ordinary man and lives a dreary life in the shadow of a peripatetic aunt. When they take a trip to Runhill Court, a house on the South Downs with ancient origins, Isbel discovers a strange uncarpeted staircase unnoticed by the others in her party. It leads up to three doors, one of which she enters (the others are opened on subsequent visits). The doors appear to represent different, heightened states of consciousness, and although they offer glimpses of a supernatural world, they are just as powerful in hinting at alternative existences. The novel is successful because Lindsay manages to keep the story almost tethered to the real world. On one level *The Haunted Woman* can be seen as a risqué romance, for in these rooms she meets Judge, the owner of Runhill Court, and the couple develop deep romantic feelings for each other. However, as soon as Isbel leaves this mysterious upper floor she is unable to remember what has happened to her. It is only during later forays up the mysterious staircase that the details of previous visits come back to her. The other-worldly strangeness of these rooms is very effective because it is juxtaposed with Isbel's ordinary, everyday life. In *Arcturus*, for example, the sudden appearance of an extra limb on Maskull's body is nothing strange, whereas in *The Haunted Woman* it is a shock when Isbel looks out of the window of a room and sees a completely different landscape to the one she had expected.

My copy of *A Voyage to Arcturus* may be an expensive first edition, bought from a book dealer friend, but if I had to choose between the two books I would retain my Gollancz reprint of *The Haunted Woman.* It has little resale value to a collector because the spine and boards are unevenly marked, faded and frayed, and inside it still has the labels from the Blaenavon Workmen's Institute Lending Department. I found it in Kim's Bookshop in Worthing (not too many miles from the setting of the book on the South Downs), on a day when I made sure to take off the shelves and inspect every book with an unreadable spine (because they are more often overlooked by collectors). It was priced at £1.50, and I am pretty sure that I talked them down to a pound – after all, the mauve oval stamp of the Blaenavon Workmen's Institute is on almost every other page. Not that I now resent the presence of the stamps – they are like ghosts from the book's past life, and as I reread *The Haunted Woman* I look forward to them making their random appearances.

*   *   *

Rosalie and I fondly recall travelling down to Maiden Newton in Dorset in 1993 for a Sylvia Townsend Warner day school with Frank Kibblewhite, and to Dorchester to the Powys Society Conference in 1995 for a STW Day. For the latter event we stayed with Janet Machen in a huge, ramshackle guest house with peacocks, and some time past midnight Janet raided the cavernous kitchen, rustling up an impromptu feast.

Over the next few years we stayed at Chydyok, visited Sylvia's old houses, and I carried on collecting and adding to the *Bibliography*. I continued to visit the exhaustive Sylvia Townsend Warner collection in Dorchester on an informal basis. We also met up with fellow STW enthusiasts Eileen Johnson and Judith Stinton.

143

And then in April 1999 Ms Y, as Sylvia Townsend Warner's literary executor, wrote to Janet to say that I had completely misunderstood her letter from 1993, and that the estate had not been against the formation of a Sylvia Townsend Warner Society after all. Janet contacted me immediately, and we resurrected our old plans.

I have a note in my diary for 14 January 2000 (Friday): 'Dorset: STW Society founded in afternoon.' To be honest, I remember it as a bit of a blur. It was a cold evening in Dorchester at the Dorset County Museum, and John Lucas gave a fascinating talk about Sylvia Townsend Warner's poetry. My abiding memory is of driving back through the dark countryside afterwards, from Dorchester to Janet's house near Shaftesbury. Janet led a convoy of cars (she was followed by Claire Harman in hers, and then me) at great speed down narrow country lanes she knew well but which were unknown to us. The celebration late that evening involved alcohol, and I slept well on Janet's sofa.

The first issues of the STW journal that Rosalie and I edited came together with a certain ease. Humphrey Stone very generously gave us permission to work our way through the engravings by his father, Reynolds Stone, from Warner's book of poetry, *Boxwood* (1960), for the front covers of the upcoming issues. We received a steady supply of interesting articles, and I knew from my work on the *Bibliography* that there was a wealth of little-known material that could be reprinted. The literary estate gave us permission to publish material by Sylvia Townsend Warner, and I was especially pleased to make available the original (shorter) ending of *Lolly Willowes*.

As a postscript, I should mention that in the summer of 2000 we moved from Sussex to North Yorkshire, and visits to Dorset became a more arduous undertaking. Once the Society was up and running and the journal established, Rosalie and I took a back seat. The Society continues today, and our admiration for the writings of Sylvia Townsend Warner is undiminished.

This is an outstanding evocation
of an age and a way of
life, but before all else
the story of a father and
son: and as such it deserves
to stand beside the
classics of that genre.

An autobiography by
ROBERT AICKMAN
GOLLANCZ

27

The Attempted Rescue

ROBERT AICKMAN

Gollancz, 1966

I already knew of Robert Aickman as an editor, but he was first recommended to me as an author in 1998 by David Tibet during a telephone conversation. The following day, all eight of Aickman's short story collections appeared in the post, courtesy of David. Rosalie and I were immediately impressed by the quality of Aickman's writing and his curiously off-kilter outlook on the world. His views are reactionary and conservative (with both a large and small 'c'), but he creates atmospheres and tensions that we had not come across in other authors of supernatural fiction. What we really enjoyed were the questions left unanswered by his stories. And so Tartarus, in association with David's Durtro Press, asked for, and received, permission to reprint the stories. The original eight books, compressed into two volumes, were published the following year and sold well. In retrospect, we should have taken more time and issued the books individually, as we did later. (Our enthusiasm got the better of us, and our first volumes were just too big and ugly.)

Over the years I have taken the time to reread and look deeper into Aickman's fiction. It is obvious that although he creates a wide range of protagonists (male and female, young and old, experienced and inexperienced), he only gives his characters *relative* autonomy. He invariably uses them to point out failings of the modern mechanised world, and our inability to accept the fundamental importance of the supernatural and the strange. Aickman was certain that there was more to the world than we normally perceive, and manifestations of the paranormal hint as to what that might be. He happily embraced evidence for ghosts, poltergeists and so on, but in his stories there is no hint of the didacticism that can spoil the fiction of other believers in the supernatural. Readers, however, shouldn't underestimate Aickman's desire to proselytise. He tried, first, in a huge and unreadable philosophical treatise, *Panacea*, that nobody would publish; second, by the creation of the Inland Waterways Association in the later 1940s, but he considered this a failure, because restoring the canal system did not bring about the national social revolution which he hoped for.

Robert Aickman spread his 'creed' most effectively, at least in terms of sales, in the interesting, though reactionary, Introductions to his Fontana series of *Great Ghost Stories* (1966–1972). He argued that the past was *always* superior to the present day; there were no modern advances worth acknowledging since the Edwardian period. However, in his fiction the message becomes almost beguiling.

It is easy to read Aickman and become immersed in the story, but the author is always present. If his protagonists can sometimes feel like puppets, they have the advantage of being controlled by a very fine puppet master. He is one of the most intelligent and articulate authors of ghostly and strange stories of the second half of the twentieth century. He may have been all but forgotten in 1998 when we first came across him, but today Aickman's stories are reprinted not just by Tartarus Press but also Faber and Faber, the New York Review of Books, Valancourt and And Other Stories (the publisher of the book you now hold in your hands).

Perhaps Aickman's most compelling and unlikely work of fiction, however, is his first volume of autobiography, *The Attempted Rescue* (1966). Draped over a framework of people, places and dates (which are not always accurately described) are colourful memories and anecdotes that highlight Aickman's role as the tragic Romantic hero. It is impossible to know to what extent he intended to mislead, for the book feels absolutely sincere. It is as much about choosing what details to include and exclude as it is about positive misdirection. One can be confident that not one word will have been committed to paper without great thought. And it was written to entertain; there is humour, although it is difficult to know how much is intentional.

Aickman tells of his dysfunctional family life. His mother is sometimes ill and pathetic, but at other times loving and strong. His father is unable to cope with family or work life, but is also godlike. Relatives and other acquaintances are defined by their oddities of character, which is rather unjust, but makes them far more interesting to read about. Aickman has various friends, but is fundamentally lonely. He does well at school, and yet never fits in. He can rightfully claim descent from Richard Marsh, the author of the Victorian shocker *The Beetle*, and uses him and other luminaries to bask in glory, sometimes from up to three removes. Aickman argued that 'magnificence, elegance, and charm are the things that matter most in daily life', but he can only see this as something that existed in the past. He is fundamentally in pain because that past is denied him.

Aickman is a snob and an unashamed elitist, who argues that he has been denied rights that he would happily refuse to others. It doesn't make him at all sympathetic, but it is obvious that his yearning to live in an idealised past must have blighted his life. One can't help feeling sorry for a man who is crippled, in many ways, by his totally unrealistic and impractical attitudes.

None of the above might seem like a recommendation to read *The Attempted Rescue*, but the picture he paints of his home life, and especially of Worton Court with his larger-than-life relatives, is unsurpassed. Macabre, wretched and bizarre, it is thoroughly entertaining.

*   *   *

In 1999, Rosalie and I visited Ladywell Cemetery in south London for the centenary of Ernest Dowson's death. We met up with Roger Dobson, who read 'Non sum qualis . . . ', and our son Tim poured a libation of absinthe over Dowson's grave, upon which, as Wilde had hoped, there were bay leaves, rue and myrtle.

Rereading *Dilemmas*, I thoroughly enjoyed 'The Diary of a Successful Man'. I can't help wondering if Robert Aickman had the story in mind when he wrote 'The Cicerones' (1968), for there are certain sad resonances with particular words, with convents, and the city of Bruges.

28

The Doll Maker

SARBAN

Peter Davies, 1953

It was also at the Aylesford Literary Conference that Mark Valentine mentioned the author Sarban to me, saying *The Sound of His Horn* (1952) was a minor masterpiece. Tongue-in-cheek, he said that he wanted to write an article called 'Sex, Sadism and Swastikas: The writings of Sarban'. Mark was attracted by the idea that a diplomat had such a secret literary inner life.

I borrowed Mark's Ballantine paperback of *The Sound of His Horn* and was very impressed by it. Mark lent me other paperbacks, and it was obvious Sarban was not only a very original author of first-rate stories, but that there was something odd and interesting going on between the lines. *The Doll Maker* struck me as the most seductive of his books – it was all about the power one man has over young women – and the story 'Ringstones' (1951) moved from exploring the idea of an individual's influence over another to more overt suggestions of physical control and even bondage. There were hints of this in his other stories, but they were subtle, and all the tales had to be read together for the recurring theme to be obvious. I told David Tibet about our new interest, only for him to send by post his copies of the first editions. To our delight, these contained extra stories not in the paperback editions.

Rosalie and I decided that Tartarus Press should publish Sarban, but we could find no information about his literary estate. Others looked on our behalf – Mark, Roger Dobson, Richard Dalby and George Locke – but to no avail. We went ahead and published *The Doll Maker* in a very limited edition of 200 copies, with a note inside to the effect that we would appreciate any information about the author. Almost immediately the American researcher Douglas Anderson got in contact to tell us he was in touch with the author's daughter, Jocelyn (Joss) Leighton. Doug generously passed on as much information as he had, revealing that the author's real name had been John Wall. I was able to write to Joss and send her a copy of our edition of *The Doll Maker*, and a few evenings later she phoned. She was very positive about the book, and to my delight said she had 'heaps of Dad's old papers'.

I was invited to visit Joss in Wales. When the bright summer day came, I allowed far too much time to travel to her secluded house, Pant-y-Cummins, in the hills beyond Welshpool, and arrived ludicrously early (long before lunch, to which I had not been invited). I found Joss sitting by her pond, drinking red wine, and together we proceeded to get very, very drunk in the hot sun. Lunch was never mentioned, and her plans for cooking a roast beef dinner that evening didn't work out, and when her boyfriend, Johnny, arrived, he did his best to catch up with our level of inebriation. Much later that night he drove us

151

around the countryside at breakneck speed to show us a house he thought I might be interested in. We woke up the owner by stumbling around the garden in search of his narrow-gauge railway, and he gave us coffee to sober us up. We got back to Joss's house long after midnight.

I left the following day with a pile of manuscripts, a crashing hangover and a doorstop beef sandwich (made from the joint we had failed to eat the previous day.) Joss had certainly whetted my appetite for Sarban, not least because her memories of her father seemed so strangely confused. She insisted that he had been distant, but then told me all about the butterflies and birds' eggs they had collected together, and which he later mounted and framed. She had also kept the toys he had made for her, the strangest of which was a wooden doll with fully articulated limbs. (Sarban was a doll maker himself.) He also built powerful crossbows, which Joss delighted in trying to use while drunk. The amount of new material and information about Sarban was almost overwhelming, but it was tantalising because hitherto there had been so few clues as to his creative life.

The first unpublished Sarban manuscript we read was 'The King of the Lake', which we published with the novella *The Sound of His Horn* to make a reasonably-sized book.

When we later published *Ringstones and Other Curious Tales*, Joss invited me and Rosalie to a celebration. We were used to taking our five-year-old son Tim everywhere with us, but from experience I knew that Pant-y-Cummins was not going to be child-friendly. Joss was very open, generous and kind-hearted, but she was also, at that time, an alcoholic.

As soon as we turned up she told us that she had arranged a surprise, and I knew there would be trouble. As the afternoon became evening we said we had to feed Tim, but Joss said she had other plans. It took a lot to get her to reveal her surprise, which turned out to be a late-night trip on a canal boat for which she had engaged a chef. We were due to be dining at about ten o'clock, which was just not possible with Tim, and a scene ensued. We received a lecture on how modern parents mollycoddled their children, and I had to tell Joss that not feeding a child until ten and then expecting them to be well behaved on a narrowboat for several hours, long after their usual bedtime, was not going to work.

Joss was upset, and despite our suggesting the compromise of Rosalie and Tim staying behind, she cancelled the boat and chef.

The next morning Joss was in a more ebullient mood, encouraging us to join her in firing off a variety of dangerous weapons in her back garden – they were mainly inherited from her father. Her mood was restored because she had come down that morning to find she had left the candles burning the previous night, and the entire surface of her varnished dining-room table had caught fire. By a miracle her old timber-framed house had not burned down, and we had not died. She decided that it was 'A good sign'.

In the last years that we knew Joss, she gave up drinking. I visited her with Mark Valentine when he decided to write his biography of Sarban, *Time, A Falconer*, and the three of us unearthed a vast amount of manuscript material, much of it fragmentary, along with diaries, ceremonial swords and his own copy of Machen's *Tales of Horror and the Supernatural*.

For a few years in the 1990s, everyone in the world of supernatural fiction fandom (readers, book dealers and presses) seemed to use as their bible the *Penguin Encyclopedia of Horror and the Supernatural*. I can state this with some certainty, because I know we did. The *Encyclopedia* contains entries not just on well-known writers but on plenty of obscure ones, and while it is now, in some respects, a little out of date, it still contains many interesting essays. The gold standard, though, is E. F. Bleiler's *Guide to Supernatural Fiction*, which was much more difficult to obtain at the time (at least in the UK), and expensive. Bleiler provides brief descriptions of thousands of novels and short stories, often (we discovered) with very accurate judgements as to their quality. Like the Machen *Bibliography*, for many years my copy of Bleiler's *Guide* was a photocopy. (I mentioned this to Everett Bleiler when we corresponded, and he thought it completely reasonable, pleased to have been such an influence on our publishing.) Another notable reference work was Donald H. Tuck's *The Encyclopedia of Science Fiction and Fantasy*. Perhaps the most idiosyncratic are George Locke's *Spectrum* volumes

29

Dromenon

GERALD HEARD

Tartarus Press, 2001

I am certain that it was in Bleiler that Rosalie and I first came across the author Gerald Heard, who wrote as H. F. Heard in the USA. Bookselling sites on the internet were in their infancy, but we managed to buy Heard's *The Great Fog* (1944), *Doppelgangers* (1947), *The Lost Cavern* (1948), *The Black Fox* (1950) and one or two other non-fiction books (rather weird and wild, which we gave away because they were not actually very good!). We enjoyed the novelty of the books turning up in the post over the following weeks from various different dealers in the UK and the USA. We take this cornucopia of choice and easy access to rare books for granted today, but I must admit that clicking 'Buy' on a website button is a little unsatisfying. I mourn the personal contact when visiting bookshops, but also telephoning specialist book dealers like Richard Dalby, Ferret Fantasy and Bistordery Books, whose printed catalogues used to come in the post.

Rosalie undertook to read all of the Heard books, making a judicious selection of the best of his stories for the Tartarus Press collection *Dromenon*. Heard (1889–1971), we soon discovered, was a curious character who wrote in a number of different genres. He was the son of a clergyman, and studied History and Theology at Cambridge but was interested in the sciences, becoming a science and current affairs commentator for the BBC. He was also a council member of the Society for Psychical Research, and in 1931 he began an informal association of engineers who looked into developing group communications, a precursor to early advances in computing. An advocate of pacifism, Heard emigrated to the USA in 1937, accompanied by Aldous Huxley. He became known there (through writing, lecturing and radio and TV appearances) as someone who promoted the interconnectedness of history, science, literature and theology. With a number of other literary friends (including Christopher Isherwood) he discovered Swami Prabhavananda and became an initiate, and in 1942 he founded Trabuco College for the study of comparative religion and various spiritual practices. Heard tried mescaline in 1954 and LSD the following year, and his conclusion was that while psychedelic drugs could provide an experience of the mysteries, they offered no obvious answers.

Apart from his philosophical books, and a non-fiction book about flying saucers (he posits the theory that they are piloted by bees from Mars), Gerald Heard wrote some very good fiction, which included three detective novels (Sherlock Holmes pastiches), a dystopian novel, an occult thriller and several volumes of short stories. In his shorter fiction his range was impressive, moving from science fiction to ghost stories with great aplomb, and his own experiences are brought to bear on often traditional themes, which is why one reviewer commented of our collection, 'Imagine M. R. James being led astray by Timothy Leary.'

The eminent M. R. James scholar Rosemary Pardoe rated very highly the supernatural tales which Rosalie included in our collection. 'Dromenon' (1944) must be one of the best stories written in any genre, employing dusty architectural/ecclesiastical details to send Professor Shelbourne off on a psychedelic trip. 'The Cup' (1948) is another apparently traditional ghost story, although it is more mystical and metaphorical, and 'The Chapel of Ease' is a confident horror piece in which a priest prays for the souls of the dead only to discover that they do not want his help. All are well-constructed stories, variations of which could have been told by James if, as the reviewer suggested, he had taken psychedelic drugs. But Heard was also the author of the wonderful 'Wingless Victory' (1944), in which a man discovers a lost avian civilisation in Antarctica, which is very un-Jamesian, and in his 'The Great Fog' (1944), mankind produces a peculiar new species that transforms the Earth's climate, but under these horrific new conditions a respect for nature is rekindled. The stories are both visionary and slightly bonkers (like their underrated and underappreciated author), and they are very effective.

In 2000 we decided to collect Oliver Onions's ghost stories for a Tartarus Press volume. Between 1900 and 1965 Onions wrote over forty novels in various genres, and many short story collections, and this work is mostly forgotten. However, his supernatural tales are still appreciated, and Rosalie borrowed from friends the books we didn't already have to make her selection. (Which means there are still gaps on our shelves, waiting for us to find them on visits to out-of-the-way second-hand bookshops.)

To obtain permission to publish the stories, I tracked down Onions's granddaughter, Jane Oliver, who told me that Onions pronounced his surname just as in the vegetable, although he did change his name legally to George Oliver in 1918. His name is unfortunate, especially for an author of such beautifully written stories. Not that it hurt his career when he was alive – he was a popular author who wrote in various genres, although only his ghost stories have really survived the test of time.

As befits the granddaughter of an accomplished author of psychological ghost stories, Jane Oliver was strangely elusive. The telephone number provided for her by a literary agent proved to be that of the Alma public house in London. At that time Jane lived in a flat above, and when I first called she came down to the phone immediately. She gave us her blessing, pleased that we were reprinting her grandfather's stories. She talked about Onions, but I had some trouble hearing what she was saying over the chatter of drinkers in the bar. The same happened when she called me to say she had received the finished book. But when I tried phoning her after this (we reprinted the collection a short while later), it became increasingly awkward to talk to her. It would take progressively longer for whoever answered the telephone to find her. Another time the phone was answered and somebody told me they would get Jane, but nobody ever came, and after straining to half-listen to a couple of bar-side conversations for fifteen minutes I had to ring off. Later I phoned and was told that there was no flat above the pub and she had never lived there. I have since found out that she died in 2013.

30

Jean Rhys Revisited

ALEXIS LYKIARD

Staple, 2000

Jean Rhys Revisited was a gift from the author Alexis Lykiard, whom I knew at the time as a customer of Tartarus Press. My copy of this chunky paperback still contains a press release and a flyer advertising the book, but, as there is no letter inside, it may have come directly from the publisher, at Lykiard's suggestion. I'm sure he sent it to me because he quotes Arthur Machen, and because he knew my interest in William Hope Hodgson, whose *The House on the Borderland* is discussed. Perhaps it was also because he complains in *Jean Rhys Revisited* that Robert Aickman was out of print, although by the time his book was published Tartarus had issued Aickman's *Collected Strange Stories.* I made a point of writing a review of Lykiard's book for the journal of the Ghost Story Society, *All Hallows*, and said that it was beautifully written, structurally poetic, and as inter-esting for what it doesn't tell the reader as for what it reveals.

I must have successfully argued to the editor of *All Hallows* that the book is about ghosts or revenants – Jean Rhys had died by the time it was written, and so had many of the other writers discussed. Rhys, while still alive, was, in some ways, a ghost, and saw her past life as ghostly. But these are real-life hauntings, because it is a book of true histories (of the author and his subject). Rhys, who had a few different careers and names, was haunted by her alternative histories. Lykiard refers to the inaccurate articles and essays about Rhys published while she was still alive, which created different versions of the same woman.

I loved the book, and when I wrote to Lykiard to tell him so he sent me a couple of volumes of his poetry, which I also admired. Although he has written novels, and Lykiard is thought of mainly as a poet, his volume of reminiscences is my favourite of his writings. It is a wonderfully unclassifiable book.

Jean Rhys, of course, is best known for the novel *Wide Sargasso Sea* (1966), written very late in her career. She led a colourful and occasionally tempestuous life, with intermittent literary success, and then, in the 1940s, she withdrew from public life, ending up in Cheriton Fitzpaine, a small village in Devon, where Lykiard made contact with her. *Jean Rhys Revisited* is many things. It is principally a memoir, not of the author herself but of the friendship between her and Lykiard, who was fifty years her junior. It is a vivid, critical 'invocation' (Lykiard's word) of Rhys, who was living in rather reduced circumstances by the time he met her. It is, in some ways, a book of rambling and digressive fragments and impressions, made more vital, honest and revealing for not having been ordered by a formal biographer. It is a writer's book, or a book for would-be writers, because it explains just how much a dedicated writer must give of themselves, and how much they must sacrifice to forge any kind of career.

Lykiard is drawn to Rhys by an admiration for her work, but also because they are both outsiders, neither having been born in Britain. He writes about Rhys, but also about himself, making interesting and accurate insights about what it is to be a creative artist.

Perhaps the single aspect of the book that has stayed with me over the years (haunted me?) is the portrait of a slightly awkward old lady living alone and relatively friendless in a small Devon village. To most of her neighbours, no doubt, she was a typical pensioner in a bungalow, unable or unwillingly to do anything about the grass that grew too long outside her front door. But, unknown to most of them, she had led a remarkable life, surviving two world wars, a literary *ménage à trois* with Stella Bowen and Ford Maddox Ford, and three marriages (one to a spy, another to a convicted fraudster). She was also the author of many well-received novels and short stories and was still, at the end of her life, passionate about writing the most vivid prose possible.

Rhys was well served by Lykiard, who keeps her alive and interesting. There is a short sequel, *Jean Rhys Afterwords* (2006), which is an effective addendum.

*   *   *

The book dealer George Locke continued to dangle in front of me the possibility of rare Machen items, which were always of an unspecified nature. I remember driving him to the Sidney Sime archive in Worplesdon, Surrey back in the 1990s. Sime had drawn the frontispiece and boards for Arthur Machen's collection *The House of Souls* (1906), and the frontispiece of *The Hill of Dreams*. George had tracked down an unpublished Sime illustration for *The Hill of Dreams* and told me that there was another unused illustration which I wouldn't be able to locate unless he accompanied me. I am certain that I could have found all four illustrations without George, but his knowledge of Sime's work meant that I got much more out of the trip than if I had gone on my own. It was worth the trouble of ferrying him to and from Guildford railway station, although it rankled a little that he stung me for an expensive lunch in a hotel over the road.

I should have known better than to agree to co-publish a book with him.

31

The House
of the
Hidden Light

ARTHUR MACHEN
AND A. E. WAITE

Privately printed, 1904

The House of the Hidden Light was long regarded by occultists as a magical text, albeit one that defied satisfactory explanation. Such was its reputation that many investigators, including Crowley, sought its key, though none unlocked its secrets. The book existed in only three copies when it was first published, and I had access to a photocopy in Newport Reference Library (which I then photocopied for myself). When I discussed it with Bob Gilbert, Waite's biographer, he admitted that he knew exactly what it was about – it was a coded record of Machen and Waite's nocturnal adventures around London, often in the company of women friends. It may not have been the great magical text so many had hoped for, but Bob's research illuminated an important period in the lives of two influential literary figures.

Janet Machen gave me permission to publish the book on behalf of Machen's estate, and Bob arranged for the rights from the Waite estate. He agreed, additionally, to write an Introduction and provide notes. Bob himself owned one of the extant three copies, but it was at that time in the hands of George Locke, who had an option to buy it from him. I told Bob that we didn't need George's input because I had my photocopy, but it was deemed politic not to mention this to George. To acquire Bob's work and the Waite rights, it was made clear I would have to co-publish with George. And so, after a convivial lunchtime meeting in The Plough on Museum Street, London, it was agreed that I would produce the book in conjunction with George's Ferret Fantasy imprint. George did subsequently discover that I had a photocopy of the text, but it proved not to be a problem. I ended up transcribing the book myself, designing it and overseeing production. I was pleased with the book 'we' published – what should have been the first trade edition of *The House of the Hidden Light*.

However, a few days before publication, while our edition was still at the bindery, George announced the publication of his own very limited-edition variant of the text. Not only had I been beaten to issuing the first edition, but Ferret Fantasy's version was a stapled booklet badly photocopied on dark brown paper that even George admitted in his catalogue was unreadable! It was also more expensive than our own printed and bound edition. When I asked George why he had done this he apologised, claiming that he assumed our edition had been published before his. And he asked me to take pity on him, saying that his mailing list was minuscule, and pointing out that his own publications never sold more than half a dozen copies. He did take sixty copies of 'our' edition (at cost price because, after all, he was co-publisher). He didn't make any effort to sell these until after we had sold out, then he offered them at twice the price, claiming the book was out of print. A few years later I discovered that he had not bought Bob's copy of *The House of the Hidden Light* after all. It is now in a museum in Amsterdam.

*   *   *

Despite a personal and professional interest in supernatural fiction, I have always read in various genres, and I keep those books that mean the most to me, often hunting down and finding collectable editions. Apart from the authors mentioned in this book, on our shelves (and much treasured in first editions) are W. Somerset Maugham's *The Magician* (1908), Evelyn Waugh's *Brideshead Revisited* (1945), Flannery O'Connor's *Wise Blood* (1952) and William March's *The Bad Seed* (1954), amongst older fiction. I have also enjoyed and tracked down first editions of more contemporary books, buying in the 1990s books such as A. S. Byatt's *Possession* (1990), Donna Tartt's *The Secret History* (1992), Louis de Bernières' *Captain Corelli's Mandolin* (1994) and Peter Ackroyd's *Dan Leno and the Limehouse Golem* (1994).

My older books have sometimes been expensive, and at other times bargains. My more contemporary fiction has often been bought at cover price. Some books have been better investments than others, but it doesn't matter to me whether they have gone up or down in value; they are all there to be read, even if doing so devalues them in the eyes of a collector.

32

Fireman Flower

WILLIAM SANSOM

Hogarth Press, 1944

William Sansom (1912–1976) was a prolific writer (like Ronald Fraser) whose many books have quietly disappeared from the shelves of second-hand bookshops over the years. I have a horrible feeling that, rather than going to appreciative readers, they may have been removed by booksellers and destroyed. It is a delicate subject, but I remember the owner of a bookshop in Norfolk once telling me about the trouble he had with his local council because he was disposing of unwanted stock in his dustbin. (The council considered it 'trade waste' and wanted to charge him.)

William Sansom's *Fireman Flower* does not deserve such a fate. For a start, it takes up little room, having been printed 'in complete conformity with the authorised economy standards' of the Second World War. Books from this period used such thin paper that they are virtually emaciated. More importantly, it is a memorable collection of short stories that showcases not just the author's fine powers of description but also his ability to create Kafkaesque fables. Some of his stories are just wonderfully odd, like 'The Peach-House-Potting-Shed' (1944). Others are moral tales, such as 'The Forbidden Lighthouse' (1944), which warns of the dangers of being seduced by pastures new, and 'Saturation Point' (1944), a wonderfully decadent tale about satiety. One of the most powerfully bleak stories is 'The Long Sheet' (1941), in which prisoners are expected to painfully wring the moisture out of a wet sheet to gain their freedom while it is constantly doused with more water – the denouement is devastating. The comparison between Sansom and Kafka is apt, as in 'The Inspector' (1942), in which a clerk loses his ticket on the bus.

But the most powerful and memorable story in the book is 'Fireman Flower' (1944). Sansom was a full-time firefighter in London in the Second World War and the story is a blend of precisely observed realism and outright surrealism. Sansom included a note at the front of the book to explain that the tale was allegorical, because the behaviour of his fictional firemen is so odd at times. The main character, Flower, is searching for the core of a fire in a vast city warehouse:

> I must pass over the fire's deceptive encroachments, and I must proceed most determinedly in search of the fire's kernel. Only in that way can I assess efficiently the whole nature of the fire.

Sansom's statement that the story is allegorical invites the reader to pull it apart and submit it to forensic analysis. Just about all of Sansom's stories are designed to say something – they are rarely merely for entertainment. It is most likely that Fireman Flower's search is a quest to understand 'the human condition'. While Sansom presents the fire realistically with a sensory overload of smoke, flame and dirty water, and the environment (at one point there is an abundance of 'great embattled cogwheels, lifeless pistons, curved shapes of rough-cast metal, stanchions'), his fireman plunges inside the warehouse without thinking of the men under his command. There are many firefighting crews already at the scene, but he rushes deeper and deeper into the building without coordination with others. When he does have a conversation with a fellow fireman, the man tries to reassure Flower that the seat of the fire has been located. Flower would like to believe it, but

Freedom from doubt, the greatest deception of all! Flower heaved his companion up onto the threshold, turned him round, and trudged back into the smoke again, pushing the man before him.

He later falls into a giant bubble bath, where other firemen have discovered a case of brandy, but Flower knows he must not yield to temptation. The next episode, just as surreal, takes him into the safety of the past. When he is about to yield to nostalgia he remembers his girlfriend, Joan, and snaps out of it. Perhaps he is suffering from smoke inhalation? The story might sometimes be too weighed down by the symbolism, but the weirdness is wonderful, and the descriptions are too perfectly worded for the reader not to want to read on.

One of Sansom's other firefighting stories, 'The Wall' (1941), is included in *Fireman Flower*, and others such as 'Building

Alive' (1946) can be found elsewhere. In fact, any collection by Sansom is worth picking up, if you can find one. In other books are the stories 'Various Temptations' (1947), about a serial killer, and 'The Vertical Ladder' (1944), in which a young man climbs a gasometer. They are always striking, and always thought-provoking.

In 2002 Tartarus published a collection of Sansom's most curious stories as *Various Temptations*, selected by Rosalie and introduced by Mark Valentine. Hopefully a few readers of our edition have saved some of the original collections from booksellers' dustbins.

*   *   *

In 1993 Rosalie and I visited Mark Valentine and his girlfriend of the time, in North Yorkshire. As Mark and I stood on the steps of Blubberhouses church, we invented a fictitious poet called Chapman Winstone Blubberhouse, and spent the afternoon imagining the details of his biography. Back at work the following week I wrote up what I remembered of this extended joke and printed a few copies, which were sent to friends. If asked, I admitted it was a spoof. However, the book dealer Ben Bass was soon advertising for books by Blubberhouse, and we thought we had better keep our heads down.

A few weeks later, I received a letter that purported to be from Blubberhouse himself. It was a wonderful letter, and I began to doubt whether Mark and I had invented him. I became even more unsure of myself when several respectable newspapers and magazines felt compelled to publish letters to their editors from Blubberhouse. It did not seem that there was any subject that he was not willing to address, whether it was

Coronation Street (the *Daily Mail*), James Hewitt and Princess Diana (the *Daily Mail*), or other varied topics of popular interest (*The Stage* and *Time Out*).

Blubberhouse was amused, no doubt, when in 1994 a Sunday newspaper asserted that he was too good to be true. The *Sunday Times* attacked the *Times Literary Supplement* for printing a Blubberhouse letter in defence of publishers' 'puffs'. He had also written to the *Sunday Times* to complain of a 'vendetta' against Jeanette Winterson, which led them to investigate their correspondent. In the letters I received from him, it was a great source of amusement to Blubberhouse that the *Sunday Times* sent someone to an address in Wiltshire to check on his authenticity. Their 'diligent' reporter could not find him at home, and thus the *Sunday Times* assumed the *TLS* had been subjected to a prank.

It was a few years later, at the funeral service for a friend, Rupert Cook, that it was revealed that Rupert was in great part responsible for the activities of Blubberhouse in the press. The final flourish for our fictional poet was a discussion of his activities on BBC Radio Four's *Home Truths* programme with the late John Peel. I hope that the show would have amused Blubberhouse, for once again it was assumed in the national media that he had never existed.

Roger Dobson's death in 2013 was a shock and a great sadness to all of us who knew him. He was passionately devoted to promoting the writers he loved, even at the expense of his own material comfort. In January 2014 Mark Valentine and I were able to look through Roger's papers, amongst which was a large folder of material about Blubberhouse, suggesting that he was equally guilty of Blubberhousing the national press.

While my confusion had been at its height, I told the story to Glen Cavaliero, who told me that for further insight I must read a certain novel entitled *Miss Hargreaves*, by Frank Baker.

33

Miss Hargreaves

FRANK BAKER

Eyre & Spottiswoode, 1940

With limited house room, there is little excuse for owning multiple copies of the same book. I do, though, feel I can justify my five different copies of *Miss Hargreaves* by Frank Baker.

I was formally introduced to Miss Hargreaves in Glen Cavaliero's own Penguin paperback, with his name written inside the front cover. It was a gift, so I cannot part with that copy. I also have a magisterial first edition of *Miss Hargreaves* in its superb dust jacket, a bargain found on an online auction site, as well as an ugly Tom Stacey reprint (because it is signed by the author). I have the Tartarus Press edition as a part of our archive, of course, but I find I also have a 1943 hardback (which will be a gift for the next person who expresses even the slightest interest in it!).

I am a great admirer of *Miss Hargreaves*, because Frank Baker created a character who is amusing and almost lovable, but later becomes threatening and dangerous without there being any real alteration in her personality. Two friends, Norman and Henry, invent Miss Hargreaves. They do this as a joke, only to discover that she has come to life. Of course, the letters she sends, threatening to visit Norman, could be a hoax, but there is a perfectly judged set piece where the young men meet her train, and the last passenger to get down from the carriage is an old lady who perfectly fits the description of Miss Hargreaves. She is a larger-than-life poetess (played by Margaret Rutherford in a stage version). At first she is a delight in every way, and her nonsense verse is delicious. The first half of the book is an uncomfortable comedy, but then Norman tells Miss Hargreaves that he wants no more to do with her. By the time she leaves the reader is on her side, but when she returns as a more autonomous individual the novel becomes very dark indeed.

Sitting alongside my copy of *Miss Hargreaves* is a rare paperback edition of the nonsense verse of Edward Lear, entitled *Margaret Rutherford Says 'How Pleasant to Know Mr Lear!'*, published by Icon Books in 1964. Frank Baker provides the Introduction, and plays the delightful but dangerous game of discussing the poems of Constance Hargreaves as though she were a real poetess. Which, of course, she might become, if one is not careful.

Baker wrote a number of other novels between 1935 and 1960, none of which were particularly successful. Most notable was *The Birds* (1936), which foreshadowed Daphne du Maurier's short story of the same name. When Hitchcock based his film on du Maurier's version of the story, Baker was aggrieved. The stars never quite aligned for him – Margaret Rutherford would have played Miss Hargreaves in a film version of his book, but the Second World War cancelled all the plans.

Baker didn't consider his writing career a success – he ended up scripting episodes of the 1970s TV soap opera *Crossroads*. But in Constance Hargreaves he created a character who would overshadow the rest of his work.

*   *   *

Although George Locke continued to mention the rare Machen items in his collection that might interest me, he didn't inform me when he offered for sale two lots of very desirable Machenalia at Bloomsbury Book Auctions in December 2005. These included the manuscript and typescript of Arthur Machen's novel *The Green Round* (1933), along with a first edition of the book, inscribed by Machen to his old friend A. E. Waite. There were also Waite's copies of Machen's *The Three Impostors* (1895) and *The Children of the Pool* (1936). The day after the sale George called me to say that I had missed out on acquiring the books, and for some reason I decided not to let him know that they had been bought on my behalf by Erik Arthur at the Fantasy Centre on the Holloway Road. In a catalogue George issued at the same time, he offered Waite's copy of *The Great God Pan* which, when I enquired, had already been sold.

It was during that phone call with George that it became my (unannounced) ambition to collect Machen's books from Waite's own library. I didn't want to admit this to George, although (or because?) I guessed he might have more himself.

All the collectors I know buy books with the idea of reading them. This might sound self-evident, but serious collectors often end up buying more than they can actually read. This doesn't negate their original intention, but inevitably there comes a time when the unread books on one's shelves seem to sit there in mute criticism.

I remember once remarking on this to Glen Cavaliero, who said that unread books are an asset, providing *potential* reading. He pointed out that a bookcase full of books you've finished reading offers no new experiences.

Sleep has his House

ANNA KAVAN

Cassell, 1948

I found Anna Kavan's *Sleep has his House* at a monthly World Wildlife Fund book sale in a lock-up garage in a backstreet in Sheffield in about 1986. I bought a whole pile of classics there in such tatty editions that, when they dried out, they disintegrated. The only books I still have on my shelves from this source are a complete works of Shakespeare (held together by Sellotape) and *Sleep has his House*.

I must have recognised Anna Kavan's name, although I don't recall from where. I had certain preconceptions about the book that I can't remember either, which meant I didn't get on with it at all, and I certainly didn't finish it. Something made me keep it, though, and it survived several house moves before being reread in Sussex in the 1990s, when I still didn't know what to make of it, and again I didn't get to the end. But some books require the reader to wait until the right moment, which was just a few years ago. I picked it up when rearranging our bookshelves and started to reread it, finally appreciating what the author was attempting. Perhaps I had previously skipped over the Foreword, in which Kavan explains:

Sleep has his House describes in the night-time language certain stages in the development of one individual human being. No interpretation is needed of this language we have all spoken in childhood and in our dreams.

It is an experimental novel of an unhappy childhood and adolescence, told through a series of dreams, each of which is prefaced by an explanation of what was happening to the narrator at that point in her waking life. She has no real friends, and though she attempts at first to fit in at school, she soon gives up. The world of the day is oppressive to her, and she survives through making a reality of the world of dreams. When she goes to university she is nearly persuaded into forming relationships, but realises that they are just shadows – reality can only be found in her interior dream world.

I had previously become bored by the book – other people's dreams, after all, are never as interesting to us as they would hope. But I finally realised that Kavan's dreams should be read as poetry, and that meant they suddenly worked for me. The dark, negative, night-time reality was beautifully and precisely described in each chapter. Understanding the artistry and care with which they had been written gave me a greater appreciation of other aspects of the book.

Sleep has his House is considered to be semi-autobiographical, a fictionalised memoir, which is problematic. Most obviously, it means that one cannot be certain what is, and is not, based on fact. For example, Kavan's mother haunts the book.

At first she is remote and sad, and then she dies under unexplained circumstances. When she is glimpsed later she is a memory, or a ghost. However, in real life it was Kavan's father who committed suicide when the author was a child. It is possible that sentiments expressed in the book are realistic, even if the details are fiction, but who knows? As a novel it does not matter – this was how the author believed she could best tell her story.

I had also understood that *Sleep has his House* was meant to have affinities with stream-of-consciousness writing. But all this suggests that Anna Kavan was not in full control of her writing, which is grossly unfair. *Sleep has his House* is finely and carefully crafted, drawing on experience but creating something that is a stand-alone work of art. Kavan is using sleep, darkness and dreams as a personal, safe space from which to try and make sense of the world of daylight. It is also a refuge. It may be her undoing, but for all its many shadows it is an astonishingly creative place.

* * *

I recently read *The Bookseller's Tale* by Martin Latham, which I would recommend for the interesting insights it has into collectors from the past, the creation of libraries, the acquisition of incunabula and the annotations that readers used to make in the margins of books (much less frowned upon in the past). One concept that Latham raised struck me as odd, though, and that is the idea of 'comfort reading'. It isn't a concept that I had previously considered because very few books that I reread are 'comforting'. Some enjoyable books make for easy, light reading, for example Nick Hornby's *Fever Pitch* (which I thoroughly enjoyed, even though it deals with Arsenal Football Club, a club I have never supported!), and *High Fidelity* (I also collect vinyl records). I also thoroughly enjoy Walter Mosley's 'Easy Rawlins' novels because they are undemanding and well written. But the lightweight nature of such books means that I don't feel a great desire to revisit them. I would rather reread a book that I didn't feel I had fully appreciated the first time round. I often want to read a book again to understand how cleverly it is plotted, or to observe how the writer has manipulated the expectations of the reader. P. G. Wodehouse tempts me to rereading, not because of the frivolous plots or even the charming characters, but because his apparently silly use of language is very clever indeed.

But, perhaps, there is one book that I do reread for comfort . . .

35

The Brontës Went to Woolworth's

RACHEL FERGUSON

Dutton, 1931

A sense of humour is entirely subjective, of course. I don't appreciate the cartoons of Thurber, but I love those by Chas Addams. Terry Pratchett leaves me cold, but Douglas Adams makes me laugh. The world would be a boring place if we all agreed on what was funny.

If I need to be cheered up I usually turn to P. G. Wodehouse, although for many years it was only the Jeeves and Wooster novels and short stories that I enjoyed. Then I realised that other Wodehouse books were just as agreeable if I imagined them to be narrated by Bertie Wooster. I can also appreciate contemporary writers such as Jonathan Franzen, but for good old-fashioned dark fun I go back several generations to writers like the deliciously cruel Saki.

However, the one book that always puts an unalloyed smile on my face, no matter which page I open it at, is *The Brontës*

Went to Woolworth's by Rachel Ferguson. It was recommended to me by Glen Cavaliero. What I really appreciate in *The Brontës Went to Woolworth's* is the ability to find yourself immediately welcomed as a guest in the house of Mrs Carne and her family, no matter at what point in the story you arrive. Even on the first page you are treated like a family friend, so there are no airs and graces and little attempt to explain that the many intimate friends they are discussing are not necessarily known to them in real life. The Carnes spend as much time imagining the details of lives of people they have never met as they do discussing their own affairs. To an outside observer, like their poor governess, this is all very perplexing. To add to the confusion, one of their imagined characters actually appears – Mr Justice Toddington (Toddy), and his wife. Inevitably, the Toddingtons do not act quite as the family had imagined, but the Carnes manage to adapt to the differences between the real and the imaginary very well, and love the Toddingtons just as much. And the Toddingtons, very generously, attempt to accommodate the Carnes' preconceptions of them.

These 'imaginary' friends are all, generally, as lively as the family who have invented them. Once Mrs Toddington understands the game she is able to report that she has recently seen other acquaintances of the family: Emily and Charlotte Brontë. They were glimpsed shopping in Woolworth's, buying 'writing-pads. And Charlotte bought a hair-net. Mauve. Quite hideous, poor girl.'

The Brontës Went to Woolworth's is entirely a light entertainment, but if one is so inclined it can lead to reflections on the power of the imagination and cause us to consider our relationships with celebrities, especially when we only know so much of them through, for example, social media. In a way unimagined by the author in 1931, virtual friends and acquaintances can assume as much reality as people we meet in real life. This is what the Carnes are doing – they glean a certain amount of information through the newspapers, and invent the rest. As far as they are concerned, they 'know' these celebrities.

But these reflections are far too pompous. Even imaginary friends can let you down sometimes, dashing your preconceptions. As Mrs Toddington was forced to admit, 'Emily had one of her difficult fits right in the middle of the haberdashery.'

Perhaps this is an example of how we like to build up our heroes, just so that they can be knocked down.

*   *   *

The Friends of Arthur Machen has thrived since the inaugural meeting at The Kings Arms in Amersham in March 1998. To make up for all the trouble I caused, I have been the Chairman in all the succeeding years. Perhaps the new Society is not as anarchic as the original, but the AGM weekends have been just as enjoyable, and are welcoming to non-members, spouses and children. My diary entry from 2007 became a report in the FoAM newsletter and gives a flavour of the meetings:

2–4 March: Machen AGM weekend in Usk. Friday saw the arrival of the advance guard at the Three Salmons – Machen's inn 'of old and happy memory'. Our esteemed Secretary Mark Samuels and his wife Adriana were already in the bar with Fantasy Centre proprietor Erik Arthur when Mark Valentine and I arrived early that evening. It was good to meet Alex Dosher for the first time. He had travelled over from San Francisco to take in the Machen weekend (and see Chelsea Football Club play). Stalwarts Gwilym Games and Mark Williams were also in attendance, and Godfrey Brangham joined us shortly afterwards. It was good to meet Bob and Barbara Mann for the first time. As usual, the conversation ranged widely over appropriate and inappropriate topics before Jon and Anne Preece arrived and we all made our usual pilgrimage to the local Indian restaurant. I seem to recall, hazily, the usual discussions and arguments over matters Machenian, along with arguments over Welsh history, association football, unpopular music, book-collecting, films, etc., etc. Back in the snug bar of the Three Salmons afterwards we were joined by Daisy Lyle, and Meic Shoring mysteriously materialised. I recall a long discussion about the weird parallel universe that is the internet, and a rarefied discussion about the warring subcultures that comprise the contemporary gothic music scene. Scarcely believable tales were related about recent book finds in Hay-on-Wye.

Because the Three Salmons was fairly quiet, the morning was a comfortably laid-back affair, and residents and non-residents alike shared a hearty breakfast before different parties formed and went their separate ways for the day. Mark Williams once again, very kindly, took a party off in his car for a jaunt around sites of local Machen interest, while another party assuaged its book-collecting habit by speeding off to Hay-on-Wye (spurred on by tales of unsorted and unpriced boxes of books littering the streets). The former party reported fine weather and splendid sights, although there were complaints of damaged footwear (!), while the latter party did indeed unearth a few unexpected treasures.

Reconvening for the AGM, business was conducted with undue haste by the Chairman as usual (members will receive the minutes in due course). We were joined by Aidan Reynolds at this point. The book auction raised exactly the right amount to pay for the wine that evening. Many thanks to the members who bid so generously, from those who later drank the proceeds with equal enthusiasm!

The annual dinner was a great success. The food at the Three Salmons is always serviceable (let's be honest, we are usually so busy talking that none of us really notice the quality), but the service was first-rate (the staff were very accommodating and friendly all weekend.) We were joined by Bridget Christie and Stewart Lee who, like other first-time attendees, obviously knew their Arthur Machen and brought interesting and fresh perspectives to conversations that, as usual, ranged far beyond Arthur Machen and his writing. At my end of the table I remember long discussions of Machen, Poe, childbirth, film (del Toro and *Ring*), the vice of book-collecting, etc. A number of us expressed pleasure at the fact that our rather 'nerdy' fascination with where authors lived, wrote and set their books, which involves visiting unremarkable addresses in dull suburbs, is now officially cool because it can be labelled 'psychogeography'.

Despite our end of the table becoming rather swampy with spilt drinks, there was enough wine left for several toasts to Arthur Machen, his daughter Janet, and absent friends, along with many other toasts that members were inspired

to propose. The official programme of events ended with
the spectacularly staged lunar eclipse (I am not sure which
member of the committee arranged this, but many thanks
to them!). [I believe it was Gwilym, the Druid Librarian.]

We retired to the snug bar once again and delighted in the
rather superb plum porter. I hope that anyone who has read
this far in my rambling account will excuse me for drawing
a veil over the rest of the proceedings – suffice it to say that
the rites of Eleusis were enacted in the rather debased form
that they have been handed down to us, and sore heads were
nursed the next morning. Many thanks to everyone who
came along and provided such excellent company.

*   *   *

Since moving to North Yorkshire in 2000, Rosalie and I meet
with friends twice a year at the York Book Fair. We also gather
together on a disorganised and very irregular basis wherever
there are bookshops to be found and a decent lunch to be had.
This is quite often (but not exclusively) in York, and I am usually one of those in our party who likes to visit the high-end and
expensive Lucius Books. Our most recent purchase there was
a first edition (1895) of *Pierrot!* by Henry De Vere Stacpoole,
bought for me by Rosalie as a birthday present. (It contains
the bookplate of the fabled musician and bookrunner Martin
Stone.) Amongst our friends, Mark Valentine tends towards
little-known twentieth-century fiction, John Hirschhorn-Smith
to decadent art, Peter Bell to books on Scotland and the Lake
District, Gail-Nina Anderson to art history, Graham Cooling
to non-fiction history, David Fletcher to fantasy artists, Paul

Chapman to Sherlockiana . . . and many others towards subjects less easily categorised. We also used to number amongst
us the late Richard Dalby (who was after ghost stories, of
course), and Malcolm Henderson (who had great collections
of Haggard and Verne). In his early years, our son Tim would
be on the lookout for Biggles books, just as I had been a gen-
eration before.

A York gathering of friends: Graham Cooling, Michelle Hirschhorn-
Smith, Mark Valentine, Gail-Nina Anderson, Joanna Valentine,
John Hirschhorn-Smith, Rosalie Parker, Tim Parker Russell

Quite often in York, the most interesting finds are second-
hand paperbacks in the Oxfam Bookshop. Although there
is a certain sport to be had in unearthing rare and obscure
books, I am well aware that there is usually a good reason why
certain books are considered 'classics'. Since moving to the
north of England I have 'discovered' many well-known authors,

reading for the first time Joan Lindsay's *Picnic at Hanging Rock*, Ralph Ellison's *Invisible Man*, Barry Gifford's *The Wild Life of Sailor and Lula*, Chinua Achebe's *Things Fall Apart* and Patrick Süskind's *Perfume* to mention but a very few. In each of the above examples I've bought a cheap paperback, fallen in love with the book, and can't help then looking out for a nicer edition (a first, if possible). There are still many classics that I have long desired and probably won't find, so the paperbacks will have to suffice.

36

The Fallen

DAVE SIMPSON

Canongate, 2008

Over recent years I have probably bought more books from Fossgate Books in York than from any other shop. Few of my purchases have been rarities, but I always find something in their stock that goes to the top of my to-be-read pile, provides great enjoyment, and is then not kept. Quite often they are books about rock bands and musicians. Most rock biographies follow the same trajectory of rise to fame, fame, and then either bust-up or decline, and appeal only to fans of the particular artists discussed. One, though, which ought to have a wider appeal is *The Fallen*, Dave Simpson's record of his quest to talk to all the many surviving members of Mark E. Smith's infamous post-punk band. In writing about them, Simpson provides an indirect portrait of Smith himself, and he is an intriguing character. He comes across as driven and focused, while at the same time a drunken, shambling mess. There is no doubt that he could be a bit of a bully, using power games to manipulate guitarists into producing exactly the sound he required. Smith took his cue from Captain Beefheart, who apparently also believed that making musicians as uncomfortable as possible resulted in them producing their best work.

Between 1979 and 2017 The Fall released thirty-two studio albums. I have to admit to being a fan, discovering them at the time of *Hex Enduction Hour* (1982) (thank you, Nick King!); I then went back and bought *Live at the Witch Trials* (1979), *Dragnet* (1979) and *Grotesque (After the Gramme)* (1980). My personal favourite has to be *The Wonderful and Frightening World Of . . .* (1984), and I first saw the band on tour promoting *This Nation's Saving Grace* (1985). I kept up with *Bend Sinister* (1986) and *The Frenz Experiment* (1988), but thereafter bought albums irregularly.

The Fall became Mark E. Smith's own personal band very early in its history. He stayed at the helm through all the changes in personnel, acting like the player-manager of a football club in which he always insisted on being the star striker. What I've appreciated about The Fall is that their music changed considerably over the years (inevitably), and Smith was always trying to do something different and innovative. He was an artist, and an avant-garde one, but he was desperate that nobody should notice this. He hated pretension, at the same time writing clever, poetic and arcane lyrics that could be considered as pretentious as hell. Peppering them with slang and offering them in a slurred Mancunian drawl was his way of insisting that he was not 'arty', really.

Mark E. Smith drank cheap lager, smoked fags and happily referenced popular culture; at the same time he was an avid reader in various genres. We know that he read Arthur Machen (he was a member of the Arthur Machen Society and wrote of Machen in his autobiography, *Renegade*), M. R. James and H. P. Lovecraft, and their influence can be seen in many of his early lyrics such as 'Frightened', 'City Hobgoblins', 'Psykick Dance Hall', 'Spectre vs Rector' and 'Leave the Capitol'. What Smith drew from such writers was the idea of being followed or haunted, manifesting in descriptions of paranoia. But Smith read more widely than this, making occasional reference in interviews to Philip K. Dick, Wyndham Lewis, William Burroughs and Thomas Pynchon.

The Fallen tells standard rock-and-roll stories of excess, onstage arguments, and the general weirdness of the world in which such performers often live, especially when on tour. Simpson discusses the bizarre ways in which some people became members of Smith's band, and how they were often unceremoniously ejected when Smith had had enough of them. Some ex-members seemed pleased that they had experienced time in The Fall, others are sanguine that the music business is often unforgiving and dog-eat-dog, while some are still bitter at the treatment they received. *The Fallen* is reminiscent of *The Quest for Corvo* by A. J. A. Symons in that it is an unconventional biography of an artist, and is all the more revealing (and enjoyable) because of the indirect portrait offered.

In the world of book-collecting, supply and demand is the major factor in determining value. A book by Stephen King that was first printed in huge numbers will still be worth more than a book that is rare but uncollected. One way of conferring additional rarity is to collect signed copies, but even more specialised, and more interesting, are 'association copies' – that is, books which have belonged to somebody, for example, who is known to have been friends with the author.

Apart from A. E. Waite's copies of Arthur Machen's books, I have managed to locate some other interesting association copies, including the author Violet Hunt's copy of Sylvia Townsend Warner's *Lolly Willowes*. For a few years Warner was in an uncomfortable love triangle with Valentine Ackland and Elizabeth Wade White, and I have first editions of Warner's *The True Heart* (1978) (ironically) inscribed lovingly to both women.

Highlights of my Robert Aickman collection are copies of *Sub Rosa* (1968) signed by the author to his agent, Kirby McCauley, and another signed to his close friend, Jean Richardson. But far dearer to me than, say, my signed Margaret Atwood and Peter Ackroyd books are the treasured association copies written by living friends that have been personally inscribed to me and Rosalie.

37

The Saint Perpetuus Club of Buenos Aires

ERIC STENER CARLSON

Tartarus Press, 2009

I first read *The Saint Perpetuus Club of Buenos Aires* in its unedited and un-typeset form on my computer. I hate reading fiction on screen, but I thoroughly enjoyed the book – it is a well-told mystery with a believable and semi-sympathetic pro-tagonist. It helped that the story involved books, bookshops and secret societies. Rosalie had already decided that Tartarus should publish it and she was sharing her discovery rather than seeking my opinion.

The novel tells how Miguel Ibañez finds part of a diary writ-ten in the margins of an old copy of *Lives of the Saints*. Although these entries would appear to be the ravings of a lunatic, Ibañez is fascinated by the idea that the author has learned how to control time. He is seduced by the thought that if he could gain such knowledge he could correct the mistakes made in his own life. When he discovers that further parts of the diary are similarly hidden in other copies of *Lives of the Saints*, he begins a quest to find them all, leading him to bookshops, abandoned buildings and the subways of Buenos Aires. This quest is set against the background of being trapped in a mediocre job at a minor government ministry, while his marriage is very realistically falling apart. I admired not only the storytelling, but also the dark satire in the layers of narrative.

The book was published, received great reviews, and we sold copies to many happy customers. In due course a paperback reprint was required, and I read this new edition while on holiday in Split, Croatia. Reading it in the early afternoons when it was too hot to leave the hotel, the book edited and typeset, I found so much more atmosphere than the first time round. The busy, indifferent city, the disordered calm of the bookshops, the painful relationship with his wife, the stifling dullness of a ministry office – it all appeared so much more vivid. While in Split we visited a bookshop, Nostrimus, at the bottom of Križeva Street, and I pictured it as Bernardo's Bookstore and Antiquary from the book, although I knew that this was fundamentally wrong – if there was a true model for the shop it was half the world away in Argentina.

And then I remembered that a fan of the book, Aschwin de Wolf, had sought out the original locations described by Carlson and had put photographs of them on his Megapolisomancy.org blog. It was all very well picturing Carlson's Argentina in my imagination and informing it through my own experiences, but with a mobile phone I was able to call up pictures of the actual building where the mysterious Saint Perpetuus was meant to have lived:

I'm sure you've seen that wonderful building while window-shopping in Barrio Norte. Its eight floors perch just above the gaudy, red canopy of the 'El Tolón' café. Up and up past all the other apartments until the cupola, a dome shingled like some ancient, grey fish. Mine is the apartment with the smallest window, all the way at the top.

It was likewise fascinating to see where Ibañez walked towards the Bulnes subway station, passing the entrance to the Alto Palermo shopping centre. On the blog I could see in detail the mural in colourful tiles by Cattaneo and Co. at the 'D' line station, and the fatal door recessed into the wall at the end of the mural.

And then I returned to the book, drawn into the quest for the diary entries of Saint Perpetuus. The images on the blog did help me picture the scenes described, although the texture and atmosphere were Carlson's own.

I reread the book recently, to write this entry, and afterwards looked up the Megapolisomancy.org blog again (the specific entry for *Saint Perpetuus* is now only accessible through the Internet Archive). I also looked up the Nostrimus bookshop on Križeva Street in Split. None of these concrete images meant anything compared to the picture created by simply reading and imagining Carlson's text. I felt as though I had entered Bernardo's bookstore at the side of Miguel Ibañez, and I could stop time, halting the action, just by closing my eyes and pausing the story. I could look around, and almost investigate the bookshelves for individual titles. I suddenly realised that if there was a real-life model for the bookshop in my mind, I had pictured a version of Bókavarðan, a bookshop I had visited in

Reykjavik which had promised a great deal, but where I had not found a single book to buy. And all this jumble of sources makes me think that research should be conducted into the interaction of our own imagination with literary texts. Of equal value would be a study of how imaginative literature affects memory. For example, a news story about Argentina came on the radio recently and I immediately pictured Buenos Aires, almost as though I had real experiences of the city. In my mind there was not just Bulnes subway station and 9 de Julio Avenue (both of which exist), but also Bernardo's bookstore (which doesn't). It took a while to realise that my only visit to the city was in the company of Eric Stener Carlson and his creation, Miguel Ibañez, on a quest for old copies of *Lives of the Saints*.

R. B. Russell, Eric Carlson and Rosalie Parker, Dublin, 2018

The Old Knowledge

ROSALIE PARKER

Swan River Press, 2010

I firmly believe that authors only play one part in bringing a work of fiction to life. The reader undertakes an equally significant role, so that when a character is introduced and is described as having a moustache or wearing a hat, an image comes to mind instantly, based on the reader's experience and imagination. Good writers are able to deftly create a fully rounded personality by explaining exactly how the moustache droops or describing the style of hat and how it is worn, just as great artists can suggest the form of a human body through a single stroke of a pencil.

When authors create characters, they usually have a physical type or particular personality in mind – even if the initial borrowing is entirely unconscious. A character may initially be inspired by an old uncle, or a young woman half glimpsed in a shop, but, almost immediately, the craft of storytelling requires that the person does or says something uncharacteristic of the source material. Perhaps the grumpy uncle has to become a friendly aunt for the sake of the plot, or the young woman in the shop becomes a pensioner so as to contrast with a child she will meet later. The alteration does not necessarily have to be a major one – the smallest of changes will distance the fictional character from the real-life model who offered the inspiration. And the same can happen with actual events and verifiable locations. This does not mean readers will not try to discover the originals of individuals and scenes in books, especially if they know anything of the author. And, of course, some writers will deliberately draw upon life and intend realistic portraits of people and places.

The author I believe I know best is my partner, Rosalie Parker. She has had four short story collections published over the last ten years, and I usually have the honour of hearing early drafts read aloud. It is because I am so close to the author that I recognise certain elements in her stories as a reflection of her own experiences. We often discuss the inspiration for her writing, and so I am able to say with confidence that I know a great deal of the background to the tales in her fine first collection, *The Old Knowledge*. I can tell you which garden, house or dale she originally had in mind as the backdrop. I might even point to real people who have counterparts in some of her tales, but offering such information would be completely misleading. Apart from, perhaps, 'Chanctonbury Ring', the locations are transmuted in Rosalie's stories so that they acquire their own life and unique atmospheres. Through the lens of her imagination, and her typically adroit and understated descriptions, they are altered to take on new resonances. Characters become their own people, quite distanced and essentially unrecognisable from those who originally suggested them.

The Old Knowledge also transforms other influences. Rosalie Parker has an affinity with and understands the techniques of the classic writers of the twentieth-century psychological ghost story. She has edited and curated collections by authors such as Oliver Onions, Walter de la Mare and L. P. Hartley. Rosalie has allowed herself to be influenced by them, while composing recognisably contemporary stories of her own.

The tales in *The Old Knowledge* vary greatly, from the clever *contes cruels* of 'The Supply Teacher' and 'In the Garden', through the darkly suggestive 'The Cook's Story', to my personal favourite, 'The Rain'. Although there are aspects of this story that I could point to as having counterparts in real life, they are essentially irrelevant. The protagonist, Geraldine, is sympathetic and believable, and so is her situation. The village in which she stays is a portrait of a particular place in the Yorkshire Dales, but of more importance is that it is a reflection of an outsider's perception of any rural community. The fundamental aspect of the story is the rain of the title: as a Yorkshirewoman once memorably declared at the premiere of *This Filthy Earth* at the Elite Cinema in Leyburn, 'They got the weather right!' Only, the weather is *not* right. The rain is relentless, and it doesn't matter if it is considered supernatural or psychological, it becomes the driving force in the story – the unremitting energy that compels the narrative to its upsetting conclusion.

It is also tempting to see something of the influence of Sylvia Townsend Warner in Rosalie Parker's stories. The two write from different times and places, but both offer the reader ordinary, if often damaged people and treat them with humanity. Perhaps the other writer one may detect as an influence is Robert Aickman – a very different author to Warner. Aickman has the ability, like Rosalie Parker, to disconcert the reader at a psychological depth that is not always obvious.

I can recommend all of Rosalie's subsequent collections: *Damage* (2016), *Sparks from the Fire* (2018) and *Through the Storm* (2020).

*   *   *

In 2011 I made a short film, starting with the pronouncement: 'I am not sure that I collect books . . .'. The positive reception inspired me to make a few more films about other book collectors, starting with Mark Valentine, whose tastes overlap with mine (Machen, Welch, etc.), but who also has other literary interests. The main aim was to share his enthusiasm for the authors he appreciates, but also to say something about his enthusiasm for collecting in general. The film has been enjoyed by a great many collectors, although Mark's cat, Percy, threatened to steal the limelight. My only regret is that, in my eagerness to film Mark and his books, a long sequence including a discussion of the Powys brothers was ruined by there being clothes drying in the background.

The third film was of the books collected by another writer, Reggie Oliver. Reggie, also an actor, always speaks well, and his interests are quite different from Mark's. Aiming for variety, I also interviewed Quentin S. Crisp. John Hirschhorn-Smith's collection of books was different again, illustrating the point that book collectors with interests in common can also have widely diverging tastes. I think the films together say something about the passion of book collectors.

I also decided to film my father, who, later in life, began collecting British cigarette packets and now has a very impressive collection dating from the 1880s through to the time when health warnings started to be printed on them. Even if one doesn't share this specific, rather niche interest, his quiet enthusiasm is very apparent in the film. It is a shame that I didn't take up his suggestion of filming another collector who lives close by, Ron Geesin, who collects spanners (an even more arcane interest!). At the local market he is known as 'Ron the Wrench' (rather than as an incredibly talented musician who worked with Pink Floyd, amongst others). Sky Arts made a full documentary about Ron and his spanners before I could.

The biggest surprise in making the collecting films, though, is that the one about my father has been far and away the most successful. I am proud of the 100,000 YouTube views for my first film, but someone unknown to me ripped off my father's video for an ASMR channel. (ASMR is a curious phenomenon whereby certain sounds, including voices, give some people an odd, almost physical pleasure.) To date my father has had over half a million views.

39

The Beetle

RICHARD MARSH

Grayson (no date)

I had heard of *The Beetle* long before I read it. The book was written by Richard Marsh and was published in 1897 as *The Beetle: A Mystery*. I had seen first editions at book fairs for eye-watering four-figure prices, but was put off buying even a cheap paperback reprint on the assumption that it would be terribly dated. It was famously published in the same year as *Dracula*, and apparently outsold Bram Stoker's classic many times over. (What is infrequently admitted is that *Dracula* was not a great success at the time of publication.) I assumed that *The Beetle* had been forgotten by all but specialist collectors because it was not nearly as good as *Dracula*.

About ten years ago I was with one of our bookish friends, Malcolm Henderson, at Keel Row Books in South Shields when I found a hardback reprint of *The Beetle*. Malcolm said it had once been his own copy, bought from a mutual friend, Richard Dalby. Malcolm was able to identify it by the evocative front panel of the jacket, which had been pasted down on the front fixed endpaper. He recommended the book – he had only sold it because he had later bought a rare early edition.

Despite Malcom's assurance that it was worth reading, it was without high expectations that I settled down with the book that evening. But Malcolm was right – it is every bit as good as *Dracula*, although it does not have all the many subsequent cultural associations that lend weight to Stoker's book. *The Beetle* is essentially about a shape-shifting Ancient Egyptian entity that follows a British politician to London, seeking revenge using the powers of hypnosis. It is told from four different, succeeding points of view, not all of which are as compelling as the first, which begins brilliantly with Robert Holt's encounter with the Beetle. Holt is not just down on his luck, but starving and in need of shelter for the night. In desperation he breaks in to an abandoned house, only to discover that, in the dark, he is not alone:

> . . . something was with me in the room. There was nothing, ostensibly, to lead me to such a conviction; it may be that my faculties were unnaturally keen; but, all at once, I knew that there was something there. What was more, I had a horrible persuasion that, though unseeing, I was seen; that my every movement was being watched.

Holt hears the creature move, and then there appear two small specks of light that he knows are eyes. The description is masterful, especially when the lights of the eyes go out, only to reappear just six inches from the floor, moving towards him. The 'Beetle' appears to be more in the form of a giant spider at this point, as Holt feels it beginning to climb up his body . . .

Perhaps inevitably, the rest of the book has trouble living up to the beginning, but it is an enjoyable novel with good momentum, and despite the melodrama it is a fine way of entering into the atmosphere of the Victorian world of hansom cabs and gaslights. It doesn't shy away from engaging with contemporary issues of unemployment and urban destitution, science, British Imperialism, radical politics, the 'New Woman' and homosexuality. It was 'of its time', and when one compares it to the original text of *Dracula*, one can see why critics tend to link the two. The faults of *The Beetle* (and there are several) are also present in *Dracula*. Why *Dracula* is remembered is that it offers a central figure of fear that suggests other possibilities than simply a horrible death.

Richard Marsh was an interesting figure. Born Richard Bernard Heldmann, he began to have boys' adventure stories published during the 1880s, but, at the height of this career, he disappeared from public view. He returned just a few years later, writing under the name of Marsh, and this second career was even more successful than the first, with the publication of *The Beetle* being the high point. For a long time nobody knew what had caused this change, but recent literary sleuthing uncovered that Heldmann had been sentenced to eighteen months' hard labour in 1884 for fraud. He adopted his new pseudonym to distance himself from his conviction.

* * *

In March 2012 I was invited to Vienna for the launch of an album of music I had recorded, *Ghosts*, which was released on Walter Robotka's eclectic Klanggalerie label. It was a delightfully surreal experience in very fine company.

I flew to Bratislava on a Friday evening, where I was met by Walter, and we were talking so enthusiastically about the plans for the next day that we mistakenly drove into Hungary from Slovakia, before turning round and heading back to Austria. Walter and his partner, Lisa, prepared a delicious dinner, and I remember us continuing talking late into the night. The following day, Saturday, was a blur, culminating in the album launch at the XI bar, which was very enjoyable, as was supper afterwards in a local winehouse.

I was not flying home until late the following day and Walter and Lisa had an important errand to run early that morning, so I stayed alone in their house in the Austrian countryside for a few hours. There were distant neighbours behind high fences, but it was absolutely still and quiet, especially after the whirlwind previous two days. It was just warm enough that morning to sit outside in the sun reading my hosts' copy of Edward Cary's *Observatory Mansions* (I had previously enjoyed Carey's 2003 novel, *Alma and Irva*). I was in an odd frame of mind, physically relaxed and caught up in the book, but I am a nervous traveller and at the back of my mind I was worried about my flight home that evening. Walter and Lisa were held up, and at noon I heard the sound of loud sirens. I instinctively knew that they were a warning of imminent nuclear attack . . .

What I didn't know was that this was a hangover from the Cold War, the siren regularly sounded at the same time every week to test the equipment.

Was this the end of the world? Would I ever see Rosalie and Tim again? I thought, if this is the start of nuclear war, at least I am comfortable and warm, and reading a good book. Ten minutes later the world had not ended, and I heard children playing somewhere far off. Another half an hour later Walter and Lisa returned, and everything was explained.

The airport was quiet that Sunday evening, and the plane half full. I remember not being at all nervous as we flew through some impressive thunderhead clouds. Believing that the end was nigh earlier that day put everything into perspective.

40

At Dusk

MARK VALENTINE

Ex Occidente, 2012

In the first few years in which we knew each other, Mark Valentine wrote a few short, interesting stories about a character called Ralph Tyler, although I mainly remember Mark's informative non-fiction articles on authors. His 1985 biography of Arthur Machen did a superlative job of placing that author in literary context.

It would not be until 1999 that Tartarus Press published Mark Valentine's first collection of fiction, *In Violet Veils*. This book records the exploits of 'The Connoisseur', an aesthete detective who only involves himself in matters occult and arcane. Every story has an original conceit, each of which is deftly handled. It seemed appropriate that Mark's first book should be designed to reflect the volumes of the 1890s, with generous typesetting and wide margins. I had been publishing for a few years, but it was not until 1999 that my experience allowed me to do his work justice. It might be my favourite of Mark's books had he not gone on to write further fiction, consistently of a comparable high quality. He often collaborates with the estimable John Howard, sharing with him such extraordinary volumes of short stories as *Secret Europe* (2019) and *Inner Europe* (2020).

Mark Valentine has also written a volume of poetry and several collections of non-fiction essays on the subject of authors, books and book-collecting. But I have chosen to write here about one of his slimmest publications, and perhaps the most obscure, *At Dusk*. In some ways it is his most uncharacteristic book – a collection of short prose poems – but it manages to encapsulate many aspects of his work, the wide variety of his interests, and his character.

Each prose poem in *At Dusk* is a homage to a different writer or poet. Mark has always been generous in admitting the influence of other writers, without imitating them. Every word is carefully selected. Each phrase is perfect and evokes a singular atmosphere or mood. *At Dusk* contains thirty-five pieces, and each is exquisite. Elsewhere, Valentine's lengthier imaginative writing contains similarly original and arresting turns of phrase, but nowhere is this concentrated in such few words. *At Dusk* is an essential distillation of his own particular writing genius. It does the book little justice to quote just one poem, for they gain their power as a sequence. From memory there are locomotives sighing, boys with lips like warm fruit, silver snakes of cigarette smoke, silent houses and footsteps like falling dice.

At Dusk is also a beautiful book physically – well designed and typeset, and illustrated by random but evocative tinted photographs by the publisher, Dan Ghetu, under his pseudonym 'Geticus Polus'. The publisher has evolved many variants of his Ex Occidente imprint, such as Exposition International, and it is impossible to collect them all – there is some debate as to whether every advertised book has actually been published. The limitations cannot always be trusted: with *At Dusk* there were 235 copies officially created, with undefined 'extra' copies for presentation. Ghetu is an artist, but his idiosyncratic attitude towards customers has caused many who would have supported him to shun his books. It is always best to obtain Ex Occidente books from the one or two intrepid dealers who stock them.

In May 2012 I was in Portland, Maine, with Todd Niemi, making last-minute changes to the script he had written for my story 'Bloody Baudelaire', which Rosalie and I had also worked on. It was about to be filmed as *Backgammon* – a title change that I still don't fully understand. There were differences of opinion between us and the director/producer which were not fully resolved before Todd and I took time off to visit Yes Books in the middle of the city. It was Memorial Day, and the parade through the town was an enjoyable although slightly surreal experience for a non-American (some of those in the parade seemed to have very distant associations with the armed forces). I was reflecting on the cultural differences between the UK and the USA as I crossed the road and was told off for jaywalking.

However, Yes Books was a haven of shared culture. I found a first edition of Murakami's *Kafka on the Shore*, and Umberto Eco's wonderful *The Mysterious Flame of Queen Loana*. I also came across a copy of Joyce Cary's *The Horse's Mouth*, which had previously come up in conversation with Todd (it was mentioned in an early version of the script). I bought him the copy as a gift, and he later reciprocated by sending me a copy of *The Hill of Dreams*, published by Knopf and probably the only edition of that book I didn't have.

I've never asked Todd what he thought of *The Horse's Mouth*. A book is a perfect gift, but it should be a rule that you don't ask the recipient if they enjoyed it. If they did, they will tell you, but you have to give them time to actually read it (up to a few years!). During that time, if they read it and their taste diverges from your own, it can be quietly forgotten.

41

Rupetta

N. A. SULWAY

Tartarus Press, 2013

In 2012 Tartarus Press received a submission that Rosalie accepted with alacrity. *Rupetta*, Nike Sulway's novel, is an alternative history, diverging from our own timeline 400 years ago when Rupetta was created, part human, part mechanical, in a small town in rural France. Rupetta's consciousness is initially tied to the young woman who has created her, and then to all those who subsequently keep her wound up. As an automaton, Rupetta is bought, sold, borrowed and ultimately revered. She is essentially immortal, and by the twentieth century everything is based on her existence, including the Rupettan fourfold law by which everyone lives.

The novel is essentially science fiction (a steampunk variant, if one allows for the clockwork mechanism that is essential to Rupetta's existence). There are also elements of the Gothic, but it is all brought right up to date by exploring ideas of love, sexuality, gender, history and power. It is immensely well crafted, and the judges of the 2014 Norma K. Hemming Award said, when it won, 'It is likely to become a classic of Australian speculative fiction, and it confirms that Sulway is a major talent.'

Nike Sulway came over to the UK from Australia for the launch of the book, which was held in the upstairs room of the Golden Fleece pub in York. The building dates from the early sixteenth century and claims to be the most haunted public house in York, with crooked stairs, low ceilings, exposed beams and creaking floorboards. It was entirely the publishers' fault (i.e. mine) that the launch was not better attended, and seeing how busy the pub was (it was a Saturday lunchtime) it was only fair that we allowed the general public to also use the room we had booked for our private function. After a fine meal, Nike stood at the head of our table and announced to everyone, including the unsuspecting general diners, that she would read from her new book, *Rupetta*. Nike held everyone spellbound and received an enthusiastic round of applause afterwards.

Despite numerous glowing reviews, more awards, and the fact that we quickly had to reprint the book to keep up with demand, *Rupetta* appears to be fading from view, which is unjust. To a very great extent literary longevity is a lottery, and one can never tell what causes a book to gain momentum or to inexplicably lose it.

Nike is a fine writer. Her follow-up, *Dying in the First Person* (2016), is a poetic and haunting story of family relationships, grief and the power of words. It is one of the great frustrations not just of publishing, but of becoming emotionally involved with great books, that you want to share the experience with other readers. It is one of the reasons why readers are always encouraging friends to follow recommendations, why people set up book clubs, and why Goodreads exists on the internet. It is why I am writing this book.

Nike Sulway at the launch of *Rupetta*

42

The Loney

ANDREW MICHAEL HURLEY

Tartarus Press, 2014

The Loney was originally submitted to Tartarus by the author in 2012 under the title 'The Green Blade Riseth'. Rosalie immediately saw its potential and wanted to publish it, but Andrew put more work into it before it returned to us, and the novel was retitled *The Loney*. It is a remarkable book, set principally in a part of Morecambe Bay (in north-west England), described by Andrew as 'that strange nowhere between the Wyre and the Lune'. Andrew has stated that he wanted to write a 'dark version of the Nativity . . . exploring ideas of faith and belief'. It is a brooding book, dominated by the dangerous landscape, and with an eccentric but believable cast of characters. Religion hangs over everything like a pall, but what makes it sympathetic and memorable is the relationship at the heart of the book between two brothers.

Tartarus Press published *The Loney* in an edition of 350 copies in 2014, and Andrew very kindly came over from Preston and signed them for us. We had to persuade our usual

214

customers to take a chance on this first novel by an unknown author, based only on our recommendation. We sent off review copies to the major newspapers as well as more indie reviewers, and even produced a video trailer. Every order for any book feels like a success, and copies of *The Loney* sold steadily, in part because of a succession of very positive small-press reviews, starting with David Longhorn at the *Supernatural Tales* blog, who wrote: 'I found it an absorbing read, with credible characterisation and an intelligent, satisfying plot that evokes the sense of mystery that abounds in the shadier, wilder parts of our little islands.' *Publishers Weekly* gave it a 'starred' review, and we became convinced that we should be able to sell out of the print run and might even have to consider a reprint. We submitted the book to the inaugural James Herbert Award (for which it was shortlisted), but not, initially, for other major awards because they require very large financial commitments that we would not have been able to meet.

Indie reviewers continued to praise *The Loney*, and then Tim Martin discussed it in an article on ghost stories in the *Sunday Telegraph*. That was when Mark Richards at the publishers John Murray asked if they could secure the rights to the book. It was quite an insight, and rather humbling, to see what a major publisher was able to achieve. Not only did Murray secure space in the windows of major bookstores and pay for adverts to appear on the walls of the London Underground, but their edition of the book scored reviews from major newspapers which had ignored it when we had previously sent copies. A large promotional budget can do a great deal for the success of a book, but in this case it was allied with Mark Richards and Murray's very genuine passion for *The Loney*.

The book won the Costa Award for Best First Novel and we went along with Andrew and his wife, Jo Shelley, to the presentation ceremony in London, where we drank a great deal of very good champagne. We spent much of the time trying to identify the celebrities who had come out for the night to do the same thing.

The Loney also went on to win both the Debut Novel and the Book of the Year at the British Book Industry Awards. It was gratifying not just that a book we had published had received such acclaim, but that such a genuinely talented writer had achieved deserved success.

43

Copsford

WALTER J. C. MURRAY

Allen & Unwin, 1948

My father asked me to find him a copy of *Copsford* several years ago, but I didn't understand at the time why he was interested in it. When Mark Valentine later mentioned the book to me, I realised it was set in the countryside around Horam in Sussex, where both my father and I had grown up.

I bought my own copy and was immediately delighted by it. The author, Walter Murray, tells how he spent a year in a derelict cottage in 1920, attempting to make a living by gathering and selling herbs. He was working alongside the wild animals and birds, with only a dog, Floss, for companionship. From the beginning, Murray has to fight not only the rats that infest his inhospitable house, and the elements outside, but also a loneliness that he finds oppressive.

Murray comes to delight in his simple life, despite its deprivations. Above all, he appreciates the wildlife he sees in meadows and woodland, the animals and insects, the birds and butterflies. He comes to a deeper understanding of plants and trees, the sun, wind, rain, frost and snow. One quote in particular stands out for me:

How careless we are about the training of our eyes to perceive colour! Day in, day out, year in, year out, what joy do we experience in the perception of exquisite colours? Only once did I ever meet a man who suggested that I should get up early one morning, as he had done on several occasions, to see colour, to see the light of the rising sun play on a particular tiled roof. It was a somewhat steeply falling roof, facing north, and only at certain seasons of the year did the morning sun glance warmly across it. Then it glowed and smouldered like the embers of a wood fire swept by the wind, with blue and violet, purple and orange flames darting about it.

The passage could have been written by Arthur Machen. Murray wrote perceptively of the natural world in a number of books, but *Copsford* is his classic of the English countryside, delighting not only in flora and fauna but in scent, colour, sound and movement. In sensitive prose Murray expresses a vivid depth of feeling for nature that makes *Copsford* a tour de force of nature mysticism.

Knowing the area Murray describes, I discovered that there were certain little mysteries and inconsistencies in his book. For example, it is not quite as isolated as he suggests, although in winter the depressions in the Wealden clay become ponds, footpaths become impassable and the river floods the fields. This would have made it necessary for Murray to take the long way round by road to reach the village, and Horam would have felt very far away. My father used to visit the site of the house from a different direction when it was even more derelict than in Murray's time. When I, in turn, roamed over the same fields I didn't even notice that a house had ever been there. As a family, we recently visited the site and found that it was easiest to go by the farm that Murray mentioned (and which my grandfather had lived in for a time). Murray claimed to have used their well for water.

We found the site of Murray's house quite easily on a warm summer day. And we discovered that it had its own well. Copsford, like the Lost Domain in *Le Grand Meaulnes*, is close at hand and yet at a great distance; it is both a real place and fictional. Murray's experiences were honestly described, and at the same time filtered through a certain amount of nostalgia and imagination. It is all the more powerful for this.

44

The Paris Notebooks

QUENTIN S. CRISP

Snuggly Books, 2017

The first book I read by Quentin S. Crisp (not to be confused with the better-known *Naked Civil Servant* Crisp) was *The Nightmare Exhibition* (2001), and I was not terribly impressed. However, almost everything he has written since this has been wonderful. Tartarus Press published his very well-received *Morbid Tales* in 2004.

Quentin deserves to be as much of a national treasure as his namesake. It is difficult to choose just one of his books to recommend, so I'll suggest one of the most obscure, *The Paris Notebooks*. This very slim volume is considered by Crisp to be an experiment in literary improvisation, forming a diary of his short time in Paris in 2007. He travelled there at the suggestion of a female friend, 'S', who provided his train tickets and a place to stay.

Crisp recorded his impressions, inner fears and general thoughts as they came to him, presumably with some idea of eventual publication. Not a great deal happens, which is often the way in Crisp's books. In his novella *Shrike* (2009), for example, his hero travels to a provincial town in Japan to stay with a widow, and thereupon meditates on the meaning of life, death and literature. Nothing actually occurs, but it is achingly beautiful. In the short story 'Sado-ga-shima' in *Defeated Dogs* (2013) the narrator and his brother walk around an island without anything of any great note occurring, but nevertheless something momentous *has* happened.

The Paris Notebooks are disconcertingly honest in practical details as well as personal and intimate thoughts, while being oddly vague. For example, he visits a Parisian cemetery, obviously Père Lachaise, but forgets its name. He can't speak French and has no money, so he can only buy occasional postcards as souvenirs. He admits that he lives on the periphery of existence in terms of financial security, literary success and sexuality. In Paris he is living even more on the edge of friendship (plans go awry when 'S' cannot come to visit him) and understanding (he resorts to mime when he wants to buy cigarettes).

At one point he muses:

I suppose I really am rather precious. Occasionally I am reminded of this fact when I find how greatly my taste diverges from the norm. These days I find that I actually wish to discard a book I'm reading if it is not precious enough . . . Action is boring. Events, for the most part, are boring. This becomes very clear indeed when one attempts to keep a diary of any sort. Jot down the events of the day, and really, as bare facts, who would ever care or find meaning in them?

However, in Crisp's world non-events have significance when he describes them. On a simple walk through the streets he finds himself unable to adequately record the architecture of the buildings (he is on the edge or periphery of communication as well), but he can still write:

> I . . . began to feel a kind of subtle intoxication, a kind of enchantment, as twilight slowly gave way to darkness. I stopped at a shop window full of differently coloured glass fashioned into ornate shapes. On the other side of the street, a strange celebration was taking place. In what appeared to be a shop emptied of furnishings and merchandise, brightly lit as if deliberately to emphasise its starkness, two little girls were laughing and chasing the balloons with which their adult playmates teased them. One young woman, dressed a little like a wedding guest, walked away from the game, as if for a rest, and lifted her dress to adjust her underwear, perhaps thinking that no one was looking. I walked on. In this light the pale façades of the buildings seemed to glow softly.

I have met Quentin S. Crisp a number of times and he is much like his books – slightly eccentric, thoughtful, insecure, but very certain of his likes and dislikes. He would never quite fit in with the literary world of any place or time, and yet there will always be the need for writers like Quentin. He looks at the world from a slightly different angle to most people, and we would do well to consider the view he offers us.

*   *   *

Brighton, 2010: Richard Dalby, Brian Showers, Daniel Corrick, R. B. Russell, John Hirschhorn-Smith, Quentin S. Crisp

The death of Richard Dalby in 2017 was a shock. Richard had been diabetic since childhood, but he took good care of himself, although I remember him turning up to a convention in Brighton in 2010 a day late because his medication had not worked. We met him at various conventions, and informally in York and Harrogate to peruse the bookshops together. I visited him at home in Scarborough, where he showed me a number of his treasured books. In 2002 he contacted me to say that he was in a quandary because he would soon no longer be able to afford one of the lock-up garages that he rented. I designed a shed for his garden, and we obtained planning permission for him.

Richard left his house and his book collection to neighbours, the Conways, who had become close friends, especially after Richard's mother died. Joe Conway had probably saved Richard's life when there had been a house fire. Joe invited me and Rosalie, Mark Valentine and Peter Bell to Richard's house to advise him what to do with all the books, and they set up Richard Dalby's Library so as to record his collection and make them available for sale. We were all astounded by the number of books Richard had collected, which made access to many of the rooms in his house almost impossible. It had not been like that when I last visited him, but we discovered that he had lost the use of his other storage garage towards the end of his life. Although his house had all the hallmarks of a hoarder's, it is obvious to me that a hoarder is not someone with too many books, but a collector with too little space.

We visited Richard's house a few times at the request of the Conways, who were, understandably, rather overwhelmed by Richard's collection. On one visit Joe insisted we take something away as a memento of Richard, and I chose his copy of Bleiler's *Guide to Supernatural Fiction* (and finally disposed of my photocopy).

45

Swastika Night

MURRAY CONSTANTINE

Gollancz, 1937. My copy:
Gollancz Left Book Club, 1940

When I was at school we were made to read both George
Orwell's 1984 and Aldous Huxley's *Brave New World*, and in
class we debated the relative merits of each book. At the time,
from my privileged position of not knowing much outside my
own comfortable cocoon, it struck me that *Brave New World*
was the more insightful book – that society would be best controlled by offering everyone what they believed they wanted. It
still seems to be a good metaphor for much that is wrong with
capitalism. 1984 struck me as too brutal – Orwell showed us
that totalitarian regimes would always inspire certain people to
fight against them. Both books are still relevant today, although
it is a shame that the science fiction elements of *Brave New
World* have dated so badly.

Various authors have used dystopias as the background to
their fiction. Many writers use the genre to make political and/
or social points, although one suspects that others use such
backgrounds rather more for the purposes of entertainment.

A popular subgenre of such dystopias takes the premise of the Nazis having won the Second World War, and an early and very strange example is Sarban's *The Sound of His Horn* (1952). This unsettling novel highlights the dangers and perversions of unchecked power, and was followed by other 'alternative histories': Isaac Asimov's short story 'Living Space' (1956), Fritz Leiber's novella *The Big Time* (1958), Philip K. Dick's *The Man in the High Castle* (1962), Len Deighton's *SS-GB* (1978), Robert Harris's *Fatherland* (1992) and Philip Roth's *The Plot Against America* (2004).

Long before any of the above examples, Katharine Burdekin (1896–1963) wrote, under the pen name 'Murray Constantine', *Swastika Night*. Burdekin's anti-fascist dystopia predates all of the above, having been written in 1935 and published in 1937 – *before* the Second World War had even begun. It was, therefore, a novel of the 'future', rather than an 'alternative history'. I had heard of *Swastika Night* (possibly through Michael Dirda) before reading about Burdekin in Chris Mikul's excellent *Biblio-Curiosa* magazine. I bought my Gollancz Left Book Club edition online, and so I have no knowledge of where it came from.

Swastika Night was inspired by Adolf Hitler's claim that Nazism would create a 'Thousand-Year Reich', and Burdekin chillingly predicted how society might appear after seven hundred years of brutally enforced Nazi philosophy. Other authors who considered the implications of German success in the war have had the benefit of hindsight, but Burdekin extrapolated from what was known of Nazi ideology at the time. It is a far darker world than any imagined by her successors.

In *Swastika Night* the supremacy of German 'blood' means, inevitably, that *all* other peoples are considered inferior, and many, such as the Jews, have been eradicated. History has been completely 'rewritten', but has to be oral because most books are banned. No other cultures are given credit as having predated that which has been created by the Nazis. The cult of Hitler has elevated him to the position of a god (legend has it that he was a seven-foot-tall blonde, blue-eyed Adonis who was not born of woman).

The novel is harrowing. It is a tour de force despite having rather a thin plot. The very nature of the world Burdekin envisages means that her characters are only able to gain a fragmentary insight of what has happened in the past, and they naturally perceive and interpret these clues with their inherited prejudice and a complete lack of knowledge of history. Burdekin does offer one small suggestion of hope by insisting that ignorance and blind, unquestioning allegiance to authority ultimately weakens those in power.

Burdekin wrote a number of other novels, often with interesting or challenging ideas. *Proud Man* (1934) has an objective hermaphrodite narrator from the future remarking upon human affairs, principally criticising contemporary gender roles. *The End of This Day's Business* (1989, published posthumously) is another anti-fascist novel offering a feminist utopia and is, again, a contemporary critique of society. These books are undeniably interesting, although they are not entirely successful as novels.

Swastika Night, however, puts all her other work in the shade. Because the dangers of fascism are present in populist politics all around the globe, Katharine Burdekin's book remains relevant today. It is a horror novel that makes anything by Stephen King or James Herbert look tame by comparison.

*   *   *

Collectors often exchange stories about those occasions on which they have found a desirable book for a ridiculously low sum. I have always thought this to be slightly distasteful – no bookseller can know the value of everything, and they have to make a living if we want to keep buying books from them. I have had a few finds like this, but for real collectors it is never really about price. (It is another matter when a bargain enables the collector to acquire a book otherwise out of their range.)

When I had little money in my teens and twenties, I developed a book collection that had significant gaps in it. (Many of Machen's books, for example, had never been reprinted in later, more affordable editions.) Paying the market price was the only way to obtain books that I really wanted. Of course, I could have spent the rest of my life waiting to find them as bargains, but then I might never have found and read them at all. For an important book a collector should expect to pay the full amount – if you are in a rush to own it – and sometimes more.

In terms of pure monetary value, the books I have purchased which have most increased in value are the ones I paid a great deal of money for in the first place (sometimes feeling I was overpaying). If making a profit is what you desire from collecting books, it is often better to buy one rarity for £1,000 than ten books for £100, or a hundred at £10 each.

46

The House of Silence

AVALON BRANTLEY

Zagava, 2017

I came very close to including William Hope Hodgson's *The House on the Borderland* amongst these fifty books, but it has never really been forgotten. Panther published at least two paperback editions in the 1960s with atmospheric artwork, and Ace published another with an equally good cover. I have all these, although I did dispense with a 1980s Sphere edition because the monster on the front was so unaesthetic. It was not quite as off-putting, though, as the Manor Books edition, which, bizarrely, shows an ear of wheat on the cover. For some time I coveted the 1946 Arkham House omnibus, but I was lucky, eventually, to find a 1908 first. Each time I bought my various copies I reread this classic work of very weird fiction – the last time was in a definitive edition brought out by Swan River Press in Ireland. The novel is an account of the narrator's time living in a very odd house in a remote part of Ireland, and of his encounters with strange creatures and experiences of even stranger dimensions. It has been called hallucinatory, and is certainly memorable. I probably saw it mentioned first in H. P. Lovecraft's essay 'Supernatural Horror in Literature' (1927).

I have also tried to read Hodgson's *The Night Land* – an altogether different experience. One can't fault the scope of Hodgson's cosmic vision: he tells of a world where the sun has died and the last members of the human race live in a huge metal pyramid, the Last Redoubt. They are under siege from various malevolent powers and forces which wait only for the inevitable weakening of human defences. As the sprawling novel begins, the narrator makes telepathic contact with the inhabitant of another, hitherto unknown, Redoubt. Of course, he goes out into the darkness to find her. The problem is that the book is dull, ill paced and with an annoying authorial voice. Added to these faults, there is a mawkish love story, so I gave away my two-volume paperback edition after slogging through only the first of them.

When, in 2017, Zagava announced the publication of Avalon Brantley's *The House of Silence*, describing it as inspired by Hodgson's *The House on the Borderland* and *The Night Land*, I bought it from the publisher with needless trepidation.

Brantley's novel is a sympathetic reimagining and expansion of *The House on the Borderland* for a modern audience, taking a great deal from Hodgson including, presumably, *The Night Land* (as I didn't finish Hodgson's original, I can't say how much!). The main character, Ashley Acheson, appears to be based on Hodgson himself, had he survived the First World War. This may sound rather derivative, but Brantley makes the source material her own, updating and, in many respects, improving upon it.

Avalon Brantley's characterisation is superior to Hodgson's. And though this is a contemporary novel, she tells the story with an old-fashioned regard to pacing, atmosphere and description, while not getting bogged down in pastiche. It is an unashamedly Gothic novel, and her prose matches her subject well. Sometimes it teeters into the overly florid and purple, but that is part of the charm, almost a part of the contract with the reader. One feels that the author isn't just telling a story, she is making it an event, and is enjoying herself:

> In the dusky light, the green-black upper branches of the forest swayed frenziedly in the wind: beaded rain rolled down the glass like thousands of tiny eyes. Far beyond the forest I could make out the moors stretching out towards the cloud-bound mountains like an unfamiliar grey horizon line. I thought of my time at sea . . .

The critic Douglas Anderson complained that Brantley's attempt to align Hodgson's cosmic concerns with Irish prehistory failed. I tend to disagree – Brantley lays solid foundations to her story, which make the wilder aspects of her novel more powerful and disturbing. But then, I never appreciated *The Night Land* because it was just too fantastic for my taste.

Sadly, Avalon Brantley passed away in 2017, aged only thirty-six, and *The House of Silence* is her only major work. This is a tragedy not just for her family and friends, but for readers of assured weird fiction. Despite its source material, much of the credit for the novel goes to Brantley herself, and subsequent novels may well have been even more confident and original. The first edition of *The House of Silence* was published in an

edition of only 170 copies, in lovely, atmospheric boards suggestive of moonlight and shadows. There is now a paperback,
which deserves a wide readership.

*   *   *

Roger Dobson's death in 2013 was a great sadness to all who knew
him. He was passionately devoted to promoting the writers he
loved. In 2014 I acquired his copy of the biography of Frederick
Rolfe, *Corvo* by Donald Weeks, not so much because I wanted
to read the book but for the letters to Roger from the biographer,
and the mass of photocopies that were tucked inside. I did not
immediately understand the relevance of the photocopies, which
were mainly of old letters, but I was intrigued by a picture of a
gun that I assumed somehow related to Rolfe.

Rereading *The Quest for Corvo* made sense of some of the
photocopies (they were of the letters written to Symons by
various correspondents when he was on his quest).

When, in 2018, we asked Mark Valentine to write an
Introduction to a Tartarus Press edition of *The Quest for Corvo*,
we hoped that it might add further interest to the book if we
were able to provide more illustrations than the four in the
original edition. It ought to be possible, we reasoned, not only
to include photographs of the various characters involved in
Rolfe's life and Symons's quest, but to track down the originals
of the letters sent to Symons.

It was Mark who pointed out that the documents quoted by
Symons had at one time been owned by Donald Weeks, and
that his collection had been offered for sale by Maggs Brothers
in 2009. A detailed catalogue had been produced, and the
Weeks material had been acquired by the Brotherton Library

in Leeds. This included, apparently, Rolfe's personal British Bulldog .45 revolver.

It struck us as intriguing that one might be able to call such a weapon up from the stacks along with a copy of *Hadrian the Seventh*. However, when we checked online we found no record of the Donald Weeks material at the Brotherton Library. It did, though, have a significant and potentially useful Rolfe collection that would be worth consulting, and an appointment was duly made for me, Mark and Rosalie to visit.

The Brotherton Library is a graceful 1936 Grade II listed Beaux-Arts building with art deco fittings, on the main campus of the University of Leeds. The hushed special collections room is modern and comfortable, and the librarians were friendly and helpful. We mentioned that we believed they had the Donald Weeks collection and, after checking, one of the librarians recalled that they did, but that it had never been catalogued. However, investigation showed that it had all been archived in a sequence that accorded with Maggs' catalogue.

Rosalie Parker and Mark Valentine at the Brotherton Library, 2018

233

We were therefore able to unearth all kinds of fascinating material, much of which was reproduced in our Tartarus Press edition of *The Quest for Corvo* (2018). Before we left, we asked if we could also see Rolfe's revolver. A member of staff disappeared obligingly into the stacks but, after a considerable time, he returned and reported that it was not to be found.

There was a possible explanation. Apparently, the library had been very pleased to accept the Donald Weeks collection, but one or two items of a rather sensitive nature had been returned as unsuitable for curation by a university library. Memories were hazy, but it was recalled that there had been some inappropriate photographs. And as for the revolver, the suggestion was that if it had been found to have been fired, then the library certainly wouldn't have wanted to keep it.

I checked with Maggs Brothers, who thought that maybe there had only ever been a photograph of the gun, although this did not accord with their meticulously described and otherwise accurate catalogue.

I wrote an essay about the missing gun in *Past Lives of Old Books* (2020), and heard back from a correspondent, Sandy Robertson, that Maggs never claimed to have Rolfe's revolver – they were only selling a photograph of it. The original weapon was owned by Weeks, but had been stolen. I suppose I should get round to telling the Brotherton Library, in case they are still looking for it . . .

47

Shadows of the State

LEWIS BUSH

Brave Books, 2018

I became aware of the Cold War in the late 1970s, by which time it was arguably at its most dangerous, although it had already been a threat for so many decades that many people had become used to it. The most compelling representations of Cold War spying and international intrigue seemed to have a period charm (Ian Fleming's *From Russia with Love* was published in 1957, Len Deighton's *The Ipcress File* in 1962, and John le Carré's *The Spy Who Came in from the Cold* in 1963). The chances of being blown up had increased by the early 1980s, but it still seemed quite unreal. I remember having to obtain special permission to see Peter Watkins's 1966 film *The War Game* in about 1983 and, of course, I was terrified by it, but at the same time it appeared old-fashioned and out of date. The school library had the wonderful *The Master Book of Spies* by Donald McCormick, but that only brought the subject up to 1973. Amongst the books I read and collected as a teenager were Ian Fleming's James Bond books, with all their 1950s and

1960s period details. (I couldn't get on with Bond's immediate precursor, H. C. McNeile's Bulldog Drummond, although I appreciated Somerset Maugham's Ashenden.)

When the Berlin Wall fell in 1989 the world realigned, but in many respects nothing really changed for those of us who do not move in political or diplomatic circles. Countries continue to distrust each other and there are tensions, diplomatic 'incidents' and invasions. The new Cold War has entered the sphere of cyberattacks using digital technology, but even today assassins still smuggle nerve agents through customs in perfume bottles, and people enter embassy buildings and are never seen again.

It wasn't until 2011 that I heard of numbers stations, an anachronistic aid to international spying that dates as far back as the First World War. The idea was simple – a very basic signal would be broadcast on short-wave radio, travelling around the globe by bouncing around the ionosphere, so that it could be heard by undercover agents abroad using nothing more suspicious than an everyday radio. All they needed to know in advance was the frequency, when to listen for a broadcast, and what any alterations or changes to the prearranged signal might mean. Some countries would play a piece of music, or a few words without any intrinsic meaning, so that nobody who was eavesdropping would understand the significance. Many countries adopted a sequence of numbers (hence the popular name), and variations or changes to the numbers gave vital information to operatives. It was the kind of technology that Ashenden or Bulldog Drummond might well have used – even James Bond in the original books. But, surprisingly, I discovered that numbers stations are still in operation today.

By surfing the internet I came across Priyom.org, which allows anyone to listen to the numbers stations that their members monitor without the need for sophisticated equipment. It is an eerie world of static, uncanny fragments of music, strange noises and disembodied voices. It is thought that some stations that still broadcast are 'ghosts' which were set up decades ago to run automatically but have been forgotten about and left switched on. Some, though, are still in active use. They have a strange fascination for the listener, hinting at a world of clandestine activity, especially when they suddenly change the time of transmission, frequency, or the previously repeated message. I became a little obsessed by the fact that they could be interpreted in many different ways by an outsider, and in 2015 they inspired me to write an album of music (*The Romance of Shortwave Radio Number Stations*, 2016), and later a novel (*Heaven's Hill*, 2022).

Priyom.org set about making the broadcasts and other material available online, but Lewis Bush decided to publish in an old-fashioned hardback book information about many of the numbers stations, including exactly where the broadcasts appeared to be transmitted. For example, the station known as 'Attención', a Spanish-language numbers station which is believed to have been broadcasting from Cuba for at least forty years, is included. Enthusiasts have used direction-finding techniques to locate the signal as coming from a communications facility outside Bauta, and Bush reproduces, in full colour, the freely available online satellite imagery that pinpoints the spot. The station known as V24, a Korean-language station believed to be operated by the South Korean National Intelligence Service, has not just been spotted by this satellite imagery, but the masts themselves can also be seen on Google Street View. The book locates stations in Britain and the USA, France, Russia, and all over the globe. Sadly, many have ceased operating in very recent years, and it is hard not to feel a slight sense of nostalgia for such low-spec technology. There is little doubt that these stations have facilitated acts against the interests of sovereign states by their enemies, but all the time they remain so shadowy they can be considered quite romantic.

I bought *Shadows of the State* online, probably from the author. It has provided the inspiration for many happy hours of poring over satellite imagery looking for broadcasting masts and installations. The trick is that masts themselves are not particularly visible from above, but they cast very long shadows. The book sits on my shelves next to a big English Heritage book, Wayne Cocroft's *Cold War: Building for Nuclear Confrontation 1946–1989*, which I bought at the York Book Fair at around the same time. It is amazing how quickly present threats are superseded and become history, but the ghosts of Cold War voices still bounce around the ionosphere, even today.

Rosalie and I have attended a few literary conventions and festivals over the years, usually taking Tartarus Press books and spending a long weekend sitting in the dealers' room behind a table. Although there is usually a good camaraderie between the publishers and booksellers offering the physical products that are the *raison d'être* of such events, we are often made to feel like 'trade'. It is additionally annoying to be considered second-class attendees when we have paid the full convention fee despite being unable to attend the talks, panels and readings. The worst of such events was probably the summer that the British Fantasy Society met at the Albion Hotel in Brighton and 'dealers' were relegated to a windowless basement where the air conditioning was not working. At BFS conventions we usually sit around until the Sunday morning, when Christopher Fowler and Lisa Tuttle appear at our stall and in half an hour make the whole event worthwhile.

Halifax, 2012: Joel Lane, Ramsey Campbell, Jonathan Miller, Reggie Oliver, Chris Priestley, Lawrence Gordon Clark and R. B. Russell, photographed by Mark Davis

We have much better memories of the 2013 World Fantasy Convention at the Metropole in Brighton, which was a triumph (many thanks to Stephen Jones and his team). The Halifax Ghost Story conventions were also highly enjoyable (thank you, Danica Ognjenovic), but by far the best event we have attended was the Dublin Ghost Story Festival in 2018. It was organised by Brian Showers, who runs the Swan River Press, and it was the model that all such events should follow.

Brian's reasoning was that, as he was organising a literary event, the book room should be the main gathering point and hub for socialising. It was closed whenever the readings, talks etc. were taking place – afterwards, everyone returned to the book room. There was a single programme, with nothing else competing for the attendees' attention, and everyone had the same experience. By luck or design, there were about 150 attendees, so everyone got to talk to each other at some point over the long weekend. It was Brian's own alchemy that got the mix of guests just right, with the wonderful Joyce Carol Oates at the head of the bill. Authors and readers were all made to feel of equal importance. It helped, of course, that Dublin is such a congenial city.

Dublin, 2018: Kathleen Shuttock, Rosalie Parker, R. B. Russell, Stuart Hale, Claus Laufenburg, John Hirschhorn-Smith and Jonas Ploeger, photographed by Michelle Hirschhorn-Smith

The Military Orchid

JOCELYN BROOKE

Bodley Head, 1948

On various occasions the late Roger Dobson recommended to me the writings of Jocelyn Brooke, and I don't know why I resisted reading the author for so long. I finally bought *The Orchid Trilogy* in a fat King Penguin edition, discovering that it collected three books: *The Military Orchid* (1948), *A Mine of Serpents* (1949) and *The Goose Cathedral* (1950). However, it was another couple of years before I found the time to read it. I thoroughly enjoyed it, with some reservations.

Jocelyn Brooke writes beautifully, in a style similar to that of Denton Welch, and with somewhat comparable preoccupations. (Brooke later edited Welch's *Journals*.) Both men were intelligent and deeply sensitive, introspective and with a slightly peculiar and personal way of observing the world around them. They both perceived themselves to be outsiders: Welch because of the injuries resulting from an accident, and because he was gay; but Brooke remains more of an enigma. They were equally unhappy at school (both ran away – twice, in Brooke's case), but they each made something lasting and positive out of a sense of nostalgia in their semi-autobiographical, semi-fictional books. They describe their discomfort in a contemporary world so personally that it invokes a melancholy wistfulness in the reader for the authors' mid-twentieth-century England, even though it probably wouldn't have been recognised by anyone else who lived through the period.

Brooke's interest in botany, especially in orchids, inspired his first book, a lyrical evocation of interior and exterior landscapes. It wrong-footed me when I first read it, because halfway through it moves on to describe the author's wartime experiences working in an army clinic for venereal disease in the Middle East and Italy. One would have thought that being a 'pox-wallah' was the worst possible situation for such a delicate soul as Brooke, but he found much to be positive about. Even though the money he earned from *The Military Orchid* allowed him to buy himself out of the army, he later decided to join up again. The camaraderie and security of the military life obviously appealed to him.

My reservations about *The Orchid Trilogy* were due to a certain repetition, not just in the three books it contains but also in his other books, including *The Dog at Clambercrown* (1955). For some time I couldn't help thinking that there were two or three perfect books that could have been made from the four. *The Orchid Trilogy* makes a certain sense as an omnibus edition, but it is to the detriment of the three books it contains.

Just a few years ago I was in the slightly unworldly Stone Trough Books on Walmgate, in York, run by the erudite but hesitant George Ramsden. It was on a day when Rosalie and I met with a few friends to make the rounds of the bookshops and visit the Blue Barbakan for lunch (at George's excellent recommendation). We were upstairs at Stone Trough Books and Mark, Graham, Rosalie and Iain were discussing with George his commissioning of twelve life-size busts of Laurence Sterne. At the back of the room I found a first edition of *The Military Orchid* in the tattered remains of a jacket, and sat on George's comfortable sofa to read it. In the calm and clear-cut light of Stone Trough Books I found myself transported by Brooke's story once again, and had to be asked if I was actually buying the book, which I did. I bought it despite having the omnibus edition, because it makes more sense as a slim volume on its own (as do the other two books). And when I read it now I am reminded not of when I first encountered it in a utilitarian King Penguin edition, but of discovering the first edition in Stone Trough Books. And I am reminded of George, who, to everyone's surprise and shock, took his own life not long afterwards.

Ave George Ramsden. *Ave* Stone Trough Books.

When George Locke died in 2019, I wrote an obituary detailing my slightly awkward relationship with him. George could be difficult and drove a very hard bargain, but my grudging respect for him turned into something close to admiration when a very unpleasant character in the book world once attempted to blackmail me. This person threatened that, unless I made public certain comments I knew to be untrue, he would send George Locke a private email from me that was very rude about George.

I phoned George and told him everything. Naturally, he wanted to know what I had written about him.

I had been so indiscreet as to suggest that George put vast amounts of research into third-rate authors and then published the results in badly produced booklets for which customers were charged unreasonably high prices. George laughed heartily, and agreed that my description was entirely accurate.

Over the fifteen years since acquiring some of George's Machen books signed to A. E. Waite, I have bought Waite's copies of *Far Off Things* (1922) and *Things Near and Far* (1923) from Bob Gilbert, who once owned a large part of the library I am still seeking. To my great delight, dealers in the USA sold me *The Great God Pan* in 2017. Sadly, I only acquired Waite's copies of *The Secret Glory* (1922), *Dog and Duck* (1924) and *The Canning Wonder* (1925) when Simon Patterson at Hyraxia Books helped to dispose of George Locke's collection after his death. I hope that George would appreciate my determination to find the books. I know there are others out there . . .

All things seem to come round in due course and find their appropriate time. I published *The Anatomy of Taverns* in 1990, but immediately discovered gaps in my knowledge of Machen's favourite pubs and published a revised second edition. I soon discovered more omissions. In 2019 I finally compiled and published *Occult Territory: An Arthur Machen Gazetteer*, with the benefit of nearly thirty years of additional knowledge of Machen and his life. I still find the man and his writing as fascinating as when I was first given the Corgi paperback of *The Hill of Dreams* by Noel Brookes in 1982. In compiling the *Gazetteer* in 2018 using my accumulated books, other historical sources and various online resources, I became particularly immersed in Machen's London of the 1880s and 1890s. I was especially interested in the bookshops that he remembered and described around Holywell Street and Wych Street, which were demolished for the Strand widening in 1900. There were a few months of intense work when I spent more time reconstructing the past than living in the present. With a friend, Mark O'Kane, I found early photos of those streets and other descriptions of them, so that I almost seem to have 'memories' of them. At the time of undertaking the research I had a dream that I was walking down Holywell Street, remarking to Rosalie that it had once been famous for its bookshops. I don't remember much about the dream, except for the atmosphere of a narrow street with its overhanging buildings, and all the windows through which I could see books.

There are times when fiction lingers in the memory longer than fact.

The Child Cephalina

REBECCA LLOYD

Tartarus Press, 2019

As a teenager I discovered a great deal of interest in *The Direc-tory of Possibilities*, edited by Colin Wilson and John Grant, an encyclopaedia of fringe thinking, 'from the Bermuda Triangle to Black Holes'. No concept was too wacky and, as I recall, the most sceptical aspect of the book was the title. One of the first entries that interested me at the time was spiritualism, because I had heard somebody discussing a local spiritualist church with a great deal of respect, despite the fact that I had been told that séances and the Ouija board were associated with the occult. I failed to see the difference – all were attempting to communicate with the dead, and none sounded believable. I was surprised to read that even the credulous Colin Wilson condemned the 'simplistic Spiritualism' associated with the Church, although he blithely attributed most observed spirit-ualist phenomena to poltergeist activity.

The book fuelled my interest in occult phenomena, although I never came close to believing in any of it – to my way of thinking, magic and the occult required exactly the kind of faith that was required by organised religions. Over the years I have never read any non-fiction written from the point of view of a believer in either God or the Devil that was half as compelling, insightful and well written as fiction that explored the same ideas.

It was therefore with great interest that I watched online as the author Rebecca Lloyd documented her research into the early days of spiritualism, wondering what she might make of it in her fiction. The result, *The Child Cephalina*, set in London in 1851, is a brilliant book written with understanding, compassion and insight. It is also very unsettling.

Lloyd's narrator, Robert Groves, is researching and writing a book on the lives of street children, many of whom he invites into his house at 12 Judd Street, where they are fed and interviewed. His intentions are entirely laudable, and his practical philanthropy is overseen by his down-to-earth housekeeper, Tetty Brandling. But everything is upset when the enigmatic and unfathomable eleven-year-old child Cephalina appears. She is not quite like the other children – for a start, she is too well cared for. Tetty is certain that there is something wrong with the girl, but Groves is fascinated by her, and discovers that she is being used in fake séances by a very dubious couple called the Clutchers. Groves hatches a plan to adopt her, although this is confused by her insistence that she has a twin sister, Euphoria, who may or may not be real. The cast of characters employed by Lloyd to tell her story are not only believable but nuanced, from the well-meaning but naive Groves to the loyal but harassed Tetty and the odd-job boy Martin Ebast. And then there is Cephalina herself – a child and therefore an innocent victim (whatever has happened to her), yet at the same time harbouring secrets and not necessarily being honest with Groves. In less assured hands there would be a very uncomfortable vein in his interest in the young girl, but Groves's naivety is convincing and his compassion believable.

As Lloyd takes us through the compelling story one is concerned for all the characters. The background of spiritualism is fascinating – especially the relationship between those who are desperate to believe and those who fraudulently exploit them. The séance described by Lloyd is particularly impressive, and the doubts that Lloyd creates are wonderfully in sympathy with those that most materialist observers would have felt at the time.

Historical fiction is difficult to write, not least because one must be in sympathy with the period in which it is set, while writing without affectation for the requirements of a contemporary audience. Writing about faith of any kind is equally fraught with danger – the author needs to have equal degrees of understanding and scepticism if they are to retain the interest of the reader. Rebecca Lloyd achieves all this with style.

In 2020, as I started compiling *Fifty Books*, the Black Lives Matter movement was having an effect on many aspects of society and culture, shaking up all manner of assumptions and prejudices. It caused me to question for the first time why so few books by writers from non-white cultures had impinged on my reading experience over almost fifty years.

When I first started buying books from the Magpies junk shop I had no idea of the ethnic background of the writers I was reading. It was only recently that I discovered that Samuel

Delany (*Babel-17*) is Black. I read Alex Haley's *Roots* without questioning why he was the only Black author in my parents' book collection. In developing a taste for modern European literature, I was embracing a tradition that was essentially white, although I was also reading American fiction, which perhaps ought to have had more representatives from diverse backgrounds. I assumed that my interest in the 1890s wasn't going to have introduced me to any non-white writers until I remembered that M. P. Shiel was of mixed ancestry.

It wasn't until the 1990s that I came across Maya Angelou's *I Know Why the Caged Bird Sings*, and the early 2000s that I read Ralph Ellison's *Invisible Man*. At some time in between these two I tried to read Richard Wright's *The Outsider*, tempted by the title, but I found it too bleak. (The anti-hero, Cross Damon, can reasonably be considered an African American 'Meursault' – the anti-hero of Camus' *The Outsider*.) When I came across a first edition of Wright's book recently I read it again, and got so much more out of it than I did the first time, when I was more interested in comparing Wright to Camus. It seems fitting in a number of ways that it is my fiftieth book.

The reason I have read so few books by writers from non-white cultures is obviously cultural, complicated and potentially contentious. All I can say is that voices from a much wider diversity of backgrounds are now available, and that can only be a very positive development.

The Outsider

RICHARD WRIGHT

Harper, 1953

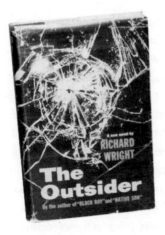

Something of the atmosphere of my first reading of this book had stayed with me – I always wanted to know what finally happens to Cross Damon. I am not sure that reading the book again has been any less soul-destroying than the first time round – it is a powerful read, but it is more nuanced than Camus' novel of the same name.

Wright suggests that all Black Americans are outsiders, and asks whether they will feel this any the less if they win the right to live 'the normal, day-to-day life of the average white American'. But Cross is not intended to be in any way representative of non-whites. He is an outsider even amongst other Black people. He mixes self-pity with a morbid introspection, believing that everything that has happened to him in life has been without his consent. Cross is certain that he has missed out on understanding the purpose of existence.

Cross is in a bad way; he is drinking too much, lives apart from his wife and children, and has got a fifteen-year-old girl pregnant. He is being squeezed for money, and there is the threat of jail. He does not know how to get out of a predicament that he acknowledges is of his own making. Then he survives a subway accident and is mistakenly reported dead. He seizes the opportunity to start again with a new identity, leaving all his problems behind. Cross hopes to make sense of the world for the first time, but he cannot change his personality. He is doomed to go on making fatal decisions.

Unfortunately, a friend recognises Cross before he can leave Chicago and, realising that he will be exposed, Cross throws him out of a window. Unlike in Camus' book, murder is motivated by self-interest. In New York Cross meets another group of outsiders, a Communist Party cell, with whom he agrees that power is everything and that the individual is nothing. But he does not accept their proposition that this is right and natural, and that it should be exploited.

He moves in with Gil and Eva Blount, and when the fascist landlord confronts communist Gil the men fight. Both are badly injured, but neither appears to Cross to deserve to continue living. He finishes them off, and though the police do not suspect Cross of their murder, another calculating communist, Hilton, does. Because he has evidence, Cross kills Hilton, once again motivated by self-interest.

Cross attempts to confess all to Eva, but she doesn't appear to take this in and they become lovers. When she later understands that Cross really is responsible for multiple murders, she commits suicide. The communists put the police on to Cross, and there follows a battle of wits between him and the district attorney.

After four murders, and having rejected politics, religion and even his family, it is perhaps through the death of Eva that Cross gains a degree of self-realisation. He is appalled by the understanding the district attorney appears to have of his character and motivations, while simultaneously craving the man's insight. Even when Cross is finally punished for his crimes, he still does not believe that he has any more comprehension of the purpose of existence.

I have seen Cross described as the opposite of Bigger Thomas in Richard Wright's better-known novel *Native Son* (1940), whose crimes are explained by social pressures. Cross is also the product of racial segregation, but he is certain that no individual in any society has any value. Arguably, Wright's 'outsider' poses more problems for the reader than Camus'. His character is far more interesting, complicated and human.

*　　*　　*

Inevitably, the Friends of Arthur Machen had to cancel the AGM weekend in 2021 due to the Covid pandemic. We were lucky to have held the March 2020 meeting in York, just a few weeks before restrictions cancelled all such events. I usually chair the AGM, and although we agreed when forming the Friends that it should be run with all the required formalities, we also decided that there is no reason for the AGM to last any longer than is absolutely necessary. As it is traditionally followed by an informal book auction, there is rarely any dissent.

Members are encouraged to donate books to the auction that they believe will appeal to other members. Some are by Machen, others relate to Machen and his circle, while others are sometimes of very tangential interest. We have sold some lovely books over the years, but in 2020 Catherine Farmer, Machen's granddaughter, donated a number of books from her grandfather's own library. (In doing so, she was generously following in a tradition established by her mother, Janet.) These books were all very desirable, and sold to a variety of different members; but there was only one that I bid on myself and was determined to win. Catherine donated a copy of *Israfel* (1886), a book of poetry, letters and 'visions' by A. E. Waite, inscribed to Amy Hogg, Machen's first wife, about whom, sadly, we know very little. As a link to a woman who is fascinating in her own right (she was a 'first-nighter' and frequented Aerated Bread shops!), the book is of great interest.

Israfel also contained Machen's own bookplate, which I had first seen in Goldstone and Sweetser's *Bibliography*, the photocopy of which had travelled around with me for many years. I had only heard of one for sale in all my years of collecting (although I never tracked it down). I also accepted a book with Machen's bookplate on behalf of FoAM, which we donated to the British Library. But here was the Holy Grail, available for the first time. Other members of FoAM knew exactly what was on offer, and there was a great deal of interest from the other bidders; but I believe they saw the determination in my eyes, and I finally acquired Machen's bookplate.

The Hill
of Dreams

A Reprise
(I now have seven copies . . .)

This novel had lost none of its power for me on a very recent rereading. Rather than being a heroic outsider, the protagonist, Lucian Taylor, now seems to be something of a snob, and a modern critic might accuse him of a sense of 'entitlement'; but he is sincere in his quest to not just be a writer, but to create worthwhile literature. And, like Ernest Dowson in 'Non sum qualis . . . ', he is faithful to the memory of his first love, Annie – in his own fashion. Above all, the quality of Machen's beautiful prose lifts the words from the page and makes reading the book a sensual experience.

The Hill of Dreams is today available as a paperback from the Library of Wales. I like to think that any popular rediscovery of this astounding novel is, in part, due to Tartarus Press reprinting it in 1998, with Janet Machen's blessing. Of course, I would never have met Janet if Adrian Bott hadn't alerted me to the existence of the Arthur Machen Society. And I would never have heard of Machen had it not been for the gift of the novel from Noel Brookes. Half of our reading life is thanks to serendipity such as this, and the other half down to the judicious recommendations of friends. It is to all these friends, past and present, that this volume of reminiscences is dedicated.